Dear Klaus and Teresa:
Merry Christmas 1989 and
Bon Appetit
Ute & Bob

Family Occasions
A·COOKBOOK

SHA '82

This book was compiled and edited by the Cookbook Committee of Concord Alternative Residence, Inc.: Diana Clymer, Marion Grabhorn, Cynthia Griffis, Ruth Johnson, Jean Sandford, Sandy Siebert, and Marian Wheeler. Illustrations are by Sue Altshuler.

From Yankee Books, a division
of Yankee Publishing Incorporated,
Dublin, New Hampshire
Second Edition (formerly titled *Main Street Menus)*
First Printing
Copyright 1984 by Concord Alternative Residence, Inc.
Library of Congress Catalog Card No. 83-51249
ISBN 0-89909-029-X

FOREWORD

Originally titled *Main Street Menus*, this book was written for the benefit of "past, present, and future residents" of Belknap House, a nonprofit congregate residence for the elderly in Concord, Massachusetts.

Its compilers sent a copy to *Yankee* Magazine's "Cookbook of the Month," a contest for cookbooks published by private organizations. *Yankee* thought it was excellent, and the book was featured as Cookbook of the Month in the September, 1983, issue of the magazine. Said *Yankee*, "Residents, friends, and board members of Belknap House have put together a wonderful cookbook . . . that brings together several generations of cooking experience and wide-ranging tastes."

Indeed, we at Yankee liked the book so much we decided to publish it ourselves, to give it a wider audience. So here it is — now called *Family Occasions*.

Clarissa Silitch
Editor for Yankee Books

NOTE: Many of these recipes call specifically for margarine rather than butter. Belknap House does this to minimize cholesterol. However, butter and margarine may be used interchangeably in all of the recipes.

BELKNAP HOUSE

The land on which Belknap House now stands was known as the "kiln lot" when John Scotchford made charcoal there in 1671. About 1838 Sewall F. Belknap came to Concord to help build the Fitchburg Railroad. Belknap bought the old General Coburn house on Elm Street, had it moved by ox-drawn sled about a mile and a half down Elm Street to Main Street, and located it on the old kiln lot. Belknap enlarged and renovated the house and lived there until 1856, when the Concord section of the railroad was completed. It was sold to William Whieldon, who further improved the property and lived there until his death.

The Edward Motley family moved to 207 Main Street in 1924. The family especially enjoyed the formal gardens planted with choice flowering trees and shrubs.

In 1976 a new organization, Concord Alternative Residence, was started by Abigail Eliot and Eleanor Fenn to establish a shared home for the elderly. The Motley house, then for sale, was ideal in size, location, and style for this purpose. Extensive remodelling was undertaken by Paul Minor, architect, and Peter Hall, builder. The heating, wiring, and plumbing were modernized, while the elegant proportions and details of woodwork were preserved. A solar hot water system was installed.

The old house acquired a new use and a new name, Belknap House. In autumn 1978 Pat and Stubb Beamis came to manage the house and welcome the first residents. Their diligent work and extraordinary skills have made Belknap House a special place. Pat excels in the culinary arts, and Stubb has produced a bountiful vegetable garden. The nine members of Belknap's family average eighty-nine years of age. The house at 207 Main Street glows with the richness of their combined experience.

CONTRIBUTORS

Ruth Backus
Barbara Bailey
Mary Bates
Pat Beamis
Janet Beyer
Eleanor Billings
Pam Osborn Brace
Bonnie Bracker
Janet Bryan
Patty Buchanan
Teeny Clymer
Mary Louise Couvillon
Bonnie Cunningham
Ann Davis
*William Davis
Bill Dawes
Helen Deacon
Caroline Dinsmore
Cindy Duncan
Carol Dwyer
Margo Euler
Gertrude Fallon
Mary Fenn
Roger Fenn
Cynthia Frailey
Lucy R. Furber
Debbie Greeley
John Hanley
Mary Hastings
Carol Hoagland
Anna Howe
Nancy James
Priscilla Jones
Lyyli Koskenhovi

*Francis Lang
Ginny Lemire
*Helen Loeffler
Patti Manhard
*Helen Marean
Carolou Marquet
Kristin Mellen-Smith
Nina Mickens
Sue Moody
Barbara Motley
Ted Motley
Mabel Paige
Ruth Piper
*Jean Prussian
Jill Reichenbach
Tess Safford
Kay Schimke
Joy Shaw
Judy Sheldon
Evelyn Shumsky
Ellen Mae-Smith
Nanlee Smith
*Arline Sosman
Margaret Stevenson
Jeannie Swaim
Marian Thornton
*Percy Thyng
Carolyn Vandam
Grace M. Walker
*Virginia Walker
Wendy Warburton
*Osgood Williams
Betsy Wilson
Meg Wilson

*Belknap House Residents

FAMILY OCCASIONS

Spring

Birthday Dinner	1
Early Spring Lunch	4
New England Supper After Sightseeing	9
April 19th Luncheon	13
Dinner Before The Concord Players	18
First Day of May Brunch	23
May Basket Supper	28
Memorial Day Lunch	32
Buffet Supper	36
After the Spring Dance	39
Porch Supper	42

Summer

Summer Brunch	46
Canoeing on the Concord River	50
Fourth of July	53
Concord Band Concert Picnic Supper	58
Rainy Day Supper	62
Summer Reunion Luncheon	66
Cool Light Supper	70
Ice Cream Social	74
Neighborhood Cookout	80
Under the Arbor Afternoon Tea	85
Out of the Garden Supper	89
Birthday Dinner	94
Labor Day Cookout	97

Autumn

Belknap House Anniversary Buffet 102
Busy Day Family Supper 107
Supper After Walking in the Estabrook Woods 110
Harvest Dinner 115
Autumn Brunch 119
Bridge Luncheon 124
Meeting Day 128
Charades Party 136
Knitting and Crocheting Tea 139
Birthday Dinner 142
Progressive Dinner 146

Winter

Sunday Dinner 154
Winter Brunch 158
Wrap a Special Present Luncheon 162
Holiday Cocktail Party 166
Fireside Supper 170
Carolling Party 173
New Year's Day Fête 178
Supper and Sing-Along 182
Home from the Hospital 186
Valentine Dinner 188
Cold Winter's Night Supper 192
Birthday Dinner 195

Spring

BIRTHDAY DINNER

Artichoke Squares

Grits Soufflé

Grilled Lamb Steak

Basil Jelly

Early Green Peas

Ginger Almond Roll

Artichoke Squares

Serves 6. Oven 325°F. 9-inch square pan, greased.

two 6-oz. jars marinated artichoke hearts, or 8½-oz. can unmarinated, drained
1 small onion, chopped
1 clove garlic, chopped
4 eggs, beaten
¼ cup fine bread crumbs
¼ tsp. oregano
2 Tbs. minced parsley
⅛ tsp. Tabasco
2 cups shredded Cheddar cheese

Sauté onion and garlic in marinade from jars, or in 2 Tbs. olive oil. Slice artichoke hearts. Mix all ingredients and pour into pan. Bake for 25 minutes. Cut into small squares. Serve either hot or cold.

Grits Soufflé

Serves 6-8. Oven 425°F. 2-quart soufflé dish, greased.

1 cup quick hominy grits
2 cups milk
2 cups water
4 Tbs. butter
2 cups grated cheese (Cheddar, Gruyère, Parmesan, or combination)
salt and pepper
pinch nutmeg
few drops Tabasco
4 large eggs, separated

Cook grits in milk and water according to package directions. Remove from heat; add butter, cheese, and seasonings. Cool slightly, and add yolks. Beat whites until stiff, and fold them in gently, ½ at a time. Bake for 25 minutes, or until slightly brown.

Grilled Lamb Steak

Serves 6.

1 Tbs. ground cumin
1 tsp. ground coriander
½ tsp. black pepper
¼ tsp. chili pepper
¼ cup olive oil
1 tsp. salt
juice of large lemon
1 large onion, sliced
2 cloves garlic, crushed
6 lamb steaks, or shoulder chops, slash edges

Mix all together and pour over lamb steaks in shallow casserole. Marinate for 2 hours. Broil over charcoal. You can reduce marinade for a sauce.

GARNISH
lemon slices

Garnish as suggested.

Basil Jelly

Yield: about 3 cups.

2 cups packed fresh, clean basil leaves
2½ cups boiling water

½ cup white vinegar
4½ cups sugar
1 envelope Certo, or ½ bottle pectin
¼ cup finely chopped fresh basil
1 drop green food coloring

Prepare an infusion by pouring boiling water over leaves. Allow to steep for several hours. Drain off infusion, reserving 2 cups of the liquid. Bring sugar and vinegar to rolling boil, and cook 5 minutes. Add pectin and 2 cups basil infusion liquid. Bring again to rolling boil for 1 minute. Cool for 10 minutes, stirring frequently. Add fresh leaves and green food coloring. Pour into sterile, hot jelly glasses. Seal with paraffin.

Ginger Almond Roll

Serves 10. Oven 350°F. Jelly-roll pan, buttered, then lined with buttered wax paper.

ROLL

7 eggs, separated
6 Tbs. sugar
¼ tsp. salt
¾ cup ground blanched almonds
2 tsp. ground ginger

Beat egg yolks until thick and lemon-colored. Add sugar gradually, and beat until pale and thick. Beat egg whites with salt until stiff. Fold yolks into beaten whites. Stir in almonds and ginger. Spread in prepared pan. Bake 15-17 minutes, or until very lightly browned. Remove from oven, and cover tightly with clean, damp cloth. Cool completely.

FILLING

1½ cups heavy cream
2 tsp. sugar
3 Tbs. finely chopped crystallized ginger
¼ tsp. almond extract

confectioners' sugar

For filling, whip cream with sugar, ginger, and almond extract until thick. Place 2 long sheets of wax paper on a table, long sides toward you, front sheet overlapping the back sheet. Sift confectioners' sugar over paper. Turn cooled cake onto paper. Peel wax paper off back of cake. Spread whipped cream over cake to ½ inch of edges. Roll cake up from the long side by lifting wax paper underneath and guiding with your hands. Slide onto serving plate and chill. Sprinkle with confectioners' sugar.

EARLY SPRING LUNCH

Asparagus Soup

Macedoine Salad

Carrot Casserole

Sour Dough Bread Sticks

Peaches in Wine Gelatin

Cardamom Cake

Asparagus Soup

Serves 6-8.

4 cups trimmed, chopped asparagus
4 cups chicken stock
3 Tbs. butter
3 Tbs. flour
1 cup cream
lemon juice to taste
salt and pepper

GARNISH

garlic croutons

Cook asparagus in stock until tender. Puree in blender, and strain. Melt butter, blend in flour, add cream, and simmer. Blend in asparagus puree and lemon juice. Reheat (do not allow to boil), and season to taste.

Garnish as suggested.

Macedoine Salad

Serves 6-8.

10-oz. package frozen peas
1 medium cucumber, sliced thin
2 Tbs. minced chives
1½ cups French dressing
1 avocado, peeled, stoned, and diced
½ cup lemon juice
½ tsp. salt
lettuce
16-oz. can pickled beets, drained

Cook peas until barely tender. Drain, and put in cold water to stop further cooking. Drain. Combine with cucumber, chives, and dressing. Marinate several hours, or overnight. Marinate avocado in lemon and salt for at least 1 hour. To serve, line salad bowl with lettuce. Arrange drained vegetables and sliced beets on lettuce in bowl.

Carrot Casserole

Serves 6. Oven 350°F. 2-quart casserole, greased.

4 slices bread
1½ cups milk
12 carrots, scraped and cooked
¼ lb. butter
4 eggs, beaten
½ cup brown sugar

Soak bread in milk. Mash carrots with butter. Mix bread and milk with carrots. Stir in eggs and sugar. Bake 1 hour or until well browned on top.

Sour Dough Starter

STARTER
2 cups white flour
4 Tbs. sugar
1 package yeast
1 tsp. salt
2 cups warm (110°F.) water

WEEKLY FEEDINGS
1 cup flour
1 cup milk
½ cup sugar

Mix starter ingredients with whisk in large bowl until smooth. Cover. Let rise in warm (80°F.) area. Stir 2 or 3 times a day for 3 days, or until mixture becomes bubbly, with a good odor of yeast. Then refrigerate, but feed once a week by adding flour, milk, and sugar. Stir down once a day until you use batter. Always take out one cupful to reserve for your next starter. Give another cupful to a friend if you wish. If the batter does not remain bubbly the yeast power is gone, so start over with a new batch.

Sour Dough Bread Sticks

Yield: 24. Oven 375°F. Cookie sheet, buttered.

1 package yeast
½ cup warm water
½ cup sour dough starter (see p. 6)
3 Tbs. sugar
1 tsp. salt
3 Tbs. vegetable oil
2 cups flour or enough to make a soft dough

egg white
poppy seeds, or sesame seeds

In large bowl, dissolve yeast in warm water. Add next 5 ingredients, and knead for 5 minutes. Place in greased bowl, grease top of dough, cover, and let rise until doubled in bulk — about an hour. Turn out onto floured board, knead a few more times, and form into 2 balls. Roll out each to 4 x 8 inches. Cut into strips ½ inch wide, and roll between palms to make long fingers. Place on cookie sheet, brush with egg white, and sprinkle with poppy seeds or sesame seeds. Let rise 30 minutes. Bake for 12-15 minutes.

Peaches in Wine Gelatin

6 sherbet glasses.

1 envelope plain gelatin **¼ cup cold water** **½ cup sugar** **½ cup boiling water** **1½ cups peach wine** **2 peaches, sliced**	Soften gelatin in cold water. Add sugar. Stir in boiling water until gelatin is completely dissolved. Add wine. Pour into glasses and chill. Add peaches when slightly set. Chill until firmly set.
GARNISH **whipped cream**	Garnish each glass with dollop of whipped cream.

Cardamom Cake

Oven 350°F. 9-inch loaf pan, greased.

½ lb. butter **1 cup sugar** **6 eggs, well beaten** **2 cups flour** **2 tsp. baking powder** **1 Tbs. cardamom powder** **1 cup white raisins** **grated rind of 1 lemon** **grated rind of 1 orange** **1 tsp. vanilla**	Cream butter and sugar. Beat in eggs. Sift dry ingredients and stir in. Fold in fruit, rinds, and vanilla. Bake 1 hour. This cake can be sliced, toasted, and served with butter.

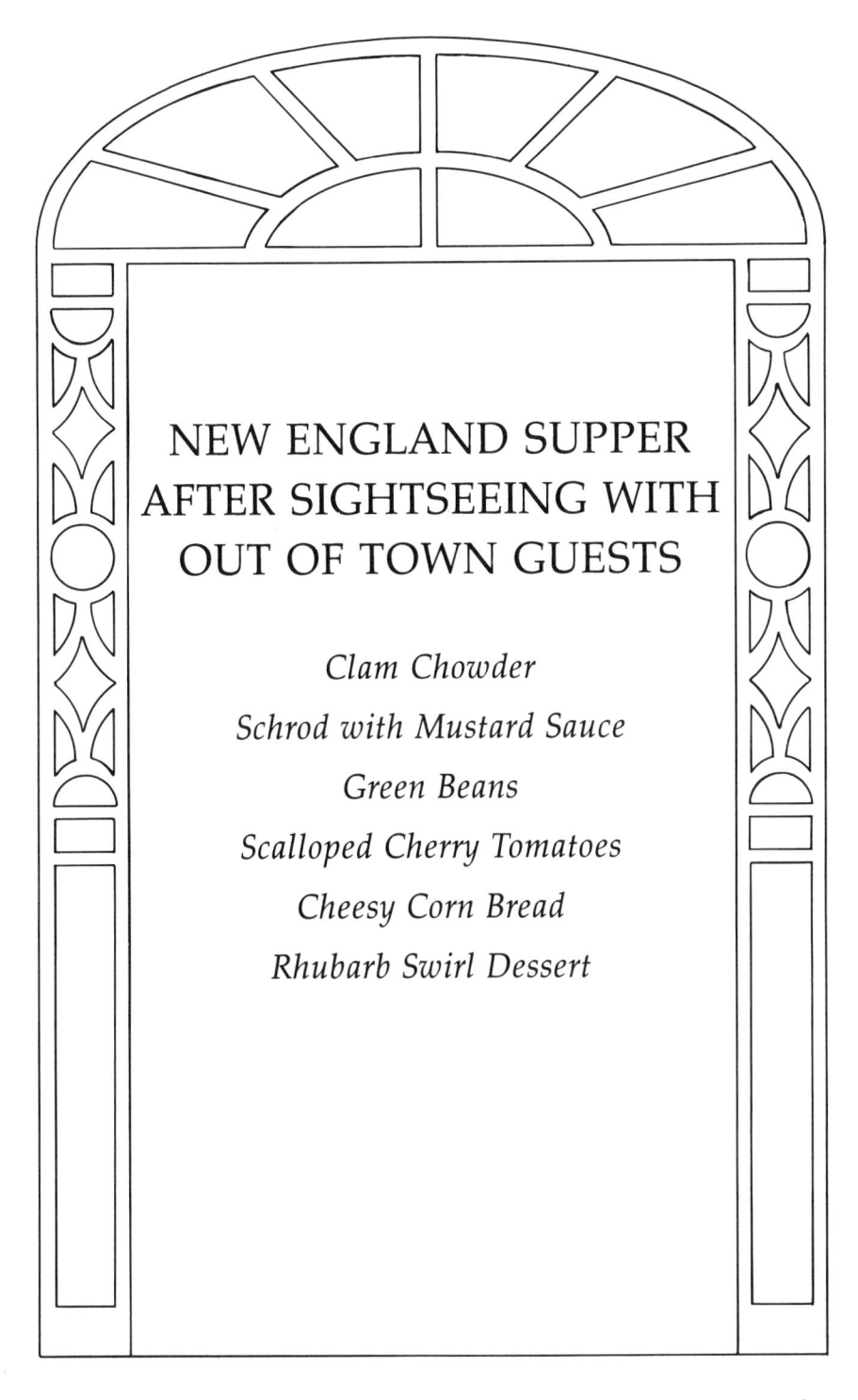

NEW ENGLAND SUPPER AFTER SIGHTSEEING WITH OUT OF TOWN GUESTS

Clam Chowder

Schrod with Mustard Sauce

Green Beans

Scalloped Cherry Tomatoes

Cheesy Corn Bread

Rhubarb Swirl Dessert

Clam Chowder

Serves 6-8.

1½ quarts (lbs.) fresh clams, about 4 cups when shucked
water

⅓ lb. fat-back salt pork

2 small onions, chopped
2 cloves garlic, finely minced
6 medium potatoes, peeled and diced
2 cups rich milk
two 13-oz. cans evaporated milk
salt and pepper to taste

GARNISH

snipped fresh dill or parsley
fried pork "scriddies"

Scrub raw clam shells with brush through 2 or 3 rinsings. Cook clams in 2 inches of water until they open — about 10 minutes. Strain off broth and reserve. Pick cooked clams from shells. If they are large, cut in smaller pieces.
Cut pork into ⅛-inch cubes and fry until golden brown. Set fried pork pieces aside. Strain off liquid fat, reserving 3 Tbs. Cook onions and garlic in this fat until golden. In a large pot, cover potatoes with water, and cook until tender — about 15 minutes. Combine all ingredients, and heat in double boiler for at least an hour, stirring now and then. If possible make this the day before serving — it is better so.

At serving time, garnish with snipped fresh dill or parsley and fried pork cubes ("scriddies").

Schrod with Mustard Sauce

Serves 6. Oven 350°F. Flat baking pan, greased.

1½ lbs. schrod fillets	Place fillets in single layer in pan.
2 Tbs. mayonnaise	Mix other ingredients, pour over fish, and bake for 10 minutes or more until tender and brown.
⅓ tsp. dry mustard	
1 tsp. Worcestershire sauce	
½ cup light cream	
salt and pepper	
parsley	

Scalloped Cherry Tomatoes

Serves 6. Oven 350°F. Shallow casserole, greased.

¼ cup olive oil	Place olive oil and tomatoes in single layer in casserole. Mix other ingredients together, and put on top. Bake for 15 minutes.
1 pint cherry tomatoes	
¼ cup finely minced onion	
1 clove garlic, minced	
¼ cup chopped parsley	
¼ tsp. thyme	
½ cup soft bread crumbs	
½ tsp. salt	
dash pepper	

Cheesy Corn Bread

Serves 6-8. Oven 425°F. 8-inch square pan, greased.

1 cup chopped onions
2 Tbs. butter
1½ cups dry Corn Muffin Mix
½ cup milk
1 egg
1 cup cream-style canned corn
½ tsp. salt
3 drops Tabasco
1 cup sour cream
1 cup grated sharp Cheddar cheese

Sauté onions in butter until golden. Set aside. Mix other ingredients except sour cream and cheese. Stir quickly. Pour into prepared pan, and top with onions, then sour cream and cheese on top. Bake until cheese is brown and bubbly — about 30 minutes.

Rhubarb Swirl Dessert

Serves 4-6.

4 cups rhubarb, cut into 1-inch pieces
⅓ cup apple or orange juice
½ cup brown sugar
¼ tsp. cinnamon
2 eggs, separated
½ cup heavy cream, whipped

Simmer rhubarb in juice until tender. Puree in blender or food processor.
Add sugar and cinnamon. Return to saucepan with beaten yolks. Stir until thickened. Cool and chill. Beat whites until stiff and fold into fruit with whipped cream.

APRIL 19TH LUNCHEON

Tomato-Carrot Soup

Dill Muffins

Tongue with Mustard Sauce

Hot Potato Salad

Jellied Beet and Celery Mold

Colonial Pie

April 19th is Patriot's Day in Concord, honoring the start of the American Revolution. The day begins at dawn with a rider representing Dr. Samuel Prescott arriving on horseback at the battlefield to announce "the British are coming." Ceremonies include a flag raising and musket salute from the Old North Bridge. Traditionally, before the parade begins, the Lions Club serves a pancake breakfast to fortify participants and bystanders. Costumed Minutemen from Concord and surrounding towns parade with many fife and drum groups, military and civic marching units. A large lunch will be appreciated by the hungry parade viewers who have been up since dawn!

Tomato-Carrot Soup

Serves 8-10.

4 cups peeled tomatoes
2 lbs. carrots, cooked
3 Tbs. butter
3 Tbs. flour
1½ cups chicken broth

3 cups milk
1 cup heavy cream
dash Tabasco
¼ cup chopped dill, or parsley

GARNISH

sour cream

Puree tomatoes and carrots in blender. Make cream sauce with butter, flour, and broth, stirring until thickened. Add sauce to pureed vegetables and stir. Bring to boil. Put in double boiler, and add milk, cream, and seasonings. Heat through. Serve with a dollop of sour cream on top. This soup is also good served cold.

Dill Muffins

Oven 400°F. Muffin tins, greased.

1 cup flour
1 cup whole wheat flour
2 Tbs. dried dill
2 tsp. baking powder
1⅓ cups buttermilk
3 Tbs. melted butter
2 eggs, lightly beaten

Combine dry ingredients. Combine liquids, and pour into dry ingredients. Mix lightly. Bake for 20-25 minutes or until golden.

Tongue

Serves 6-8.

3 lbs. fresh or smoked tongue
1 bay leaf
a few peppercorns
parsley, thyme
minced onions

Simmer tongue in water with seasonings for 3 hours. Remove outside skin before serving.

Mustard Sauce

Yield: about 1 cup.

3 egg yolks
½ lb. melted butter
2 tsp. vinegar
1 Tbs. horseradish
¼ tsp. salt
1 tsp. Dijon mustard

Using blender, blend egg yolks until foamy. Add butter in steady stream, blending on medium speed. Blend in vinegar, horseradish, salt, and mustard. Serve with hot tongue.

Sour Cream Horseradish Sauce

Yield: about 1 cup.

1 cup sour cream
1 tsp. dry mustard
2 Tbs. horseradish
1 Tbs. chopped scallions
1 Tbs. chopped dill

Mix all ingredients together until smooth.

Serve with tongue, cold meat, or fish.

Hot Potato Salad

Serves 8.

8 medium potatoes
6 strips bacon, diced
½ cup chopped onion
½ cup chopped celery
½ cup vinegar
⅓ cup water
2 Tbs. sugar
½ tsp. salt
½ tsp. dry mustard

GARNISH
chopped parsley

Boil potatoes with jackets on until tender. Remove skins, and slice into bowl. Fry bacon, and drain on paper. To bacon fat in skillet, add onion and celery, and sauté lightly. Add vinegar, water, and seasonings to skillet, and heat through. Pour over potatoes and toss. Sprinkle with bacon bits, and garnish with parsley. Serve warm or cold.

Jellied Beet and Celery Mold

Serves 4.

1 Tbs. plain gelatin
⅓ cup cold water
½ cup beet juice, heated
2 Tbs. sugar
2½ Tbs. lemon juice
1½ tsp. prepared horseradish
½ tsp. salt
pepper
1 cup diced cooked beets
¼ cup finely chopped celery

Soften gelatin in water. Dissolve in hot beet juice. Add remaining ingredients. Chill until set.

Colonial Pie

Serves 6-8. Oven 350°F. 9-inch pie pan.

PASTRY

⅓ cup lard, or ⅓ cup plus 1 Tbs. shortening
1 cup flour
½ tsp. salt
2 Tbs. cold water

Cut lard or shortening into combined flour and salt. Add cold water to make pastry. Line pan with pastry, fluting sides high. Set aside while preparing sauce and batter.

SAUCE

1½ squares unsweetened chocolate
½ cup water
⅔ cup sugar
¼ cup butter
1½ tsp. vanilla

Melt chocolate with water in double boiler. Remove bottom half, and add sugar to mixture in top half of double boiler. Bring to boil, stirring constantly. Remove from heat. Stir in butter and vanilla. Set aside.

BATTER

1 cup flour
¾ cup sugar
1 tsp. baking powder
½ tsp. salt
½ cup milk
¼ cup shortening
½ tsp. vanilla
1 egg
½ cup finely chopped nuts

Sift dry ingredients together. Add milk, shortening, and vanilla, and beat 2 minutes. Add egg, and beat for 2 minutes. Pour into pie crust. Stir sauce, reheating if necessary to make it pourable, and pour carefully over batter. Sprinkle top with nuts. Bake 55-60 minutes, or until toothpick comes out clean.

GARNISH

whipped cream, or ice cream

Serve with whipped cream or ice cream.

DINNER BEFORE THE CONCORD PLAYERS

Danish Liver Pâté

Pasta al Forno

Sour Dough Bread

Green Salad

Cold Lemon Soufflé

Danish Liver Pâté

Serves 8-12. Oven 350°F. Loaf pan.

WHITE SAUCE

2 Tbs. butter
2 Tbs. flour
⅔ cup medium cream
½ cup milk

Melt butter, stir in flour, cook 2 minutes, then gradually add cream and milk, stirring constantly until thickened. Cool.

PÂTÉ

1 lb. bacon
1 lb. fresh liver — pork, beef, calf, or chicken
⅓ lb. fresh pork fat, or salt pork soaked in cold water for 1 hour
1 medium onion
2 Tbs. dry sherry
2 eggs
1½ tsp. salt (omit if using salt pork)
¾ tsp. white pepper
½ tsp. allspice
½ tsp. ground cloves

Line pan with overlapping strips of bacon. Let bacon lengths hang over sides. Remove any membranes or fatty tissue from liver. Cut liver, fat and onion into chunks and put through meat grinder, or puree in blender, in several batches. Add white sauce and sherry to liver. Beat eggs with salt and spices. Mix well with liver mixture. Pour into bacon-lined pan, and fold overhanging bacon over top. Cover pan tightly with 2 thicknesses of foil, and seal edges. Place in large pan with water reaching at least ⅓ way up sides of pan. Bake for 1½ hours. Remove foil to cool, but replace to chill. Serve chilled, with rye bread and crackers.

Pasta Al Forno

Serves 8-12. Oven 350°F. 9 x 13-inch pan, greased.

- ½ lb. rigatoni
- 1½ lbs. zucchini, unpeeled
- 1 large onion, sliced thinly
- ½ lb. potatoes, sliced thinly
- ¼ lb. margarine
- 1 cup prosciutto, or smoked ham strips
- 1 lb. tomatoes, peeled and chopped, or 2 cups drained canned tomatoes
- ⅔ cup minced parsley
- ⅓ cup chopped fresh basil, or 1-2 Tbs. dried
- salt and pepper
- ¾ cup freshly grated Parmesan cheese

Cook rigatoni in salted water and drain. Cut zucchini in thin, lengthwise strips, place in colander, and sprinkle with salt. Let stand 30 minutes, then squeeze dry between paper towels. Line pan with zucchini; then add layers in this order: onion, potatoes, 2 Tbs. margarine dotted in, ham strips, 2 Tbs. margarine, rigatoni, 2 Tbs. margarine, tomatoes, parsley, basil, salt, pepper, and cheese. Dot with remaining margarine. Cover and bake for 45 minutes to 1 hour. This is an economical dish for a big crowd.

Sour Dough Bread

Yield: 2 loaves. Oven 400°F. Two 9-inch loaf pans, or French bread pans, greased.

SPONGE

- 1 cup warm water
- 1 cup sourdough starter (see p.6)
- 2 Tbs. sugar
- 3 cups flour
- 1 tsp. salt

To prepare sponge, mix first ingredients several hours before baking time. Allow to double in bulk.

TO FINISH

- ½ cup warm water
- 1 envelope yeast
- 1 cup flour
- 1½ or 2 cups additional flour

Dissolve yeast in warm water. Add flour; beat well. Add to sponge, and turn out on floured board. Knead in enough flour to make a stiff dough.

Place in greased bowl, grease top, cover, and let rise until double, about 2 hours. Punch down, and let rise again — about 45 minutes. Knead again, and divide dough into 2 pans. Allow to rise 1 hour.

Bake for 40 minutes in preheated oven with a shallow pan of boiling water on lowest rack, bread pans above them. When done, loaves make a hollow sound when tapped. Invert loaves on rack to cool.

Green Salad

mixed greens: endive, chicory, romaine
raw mushrooms, sliced
red onions, sliced

Toss greens, mushrooms, and onions together.

ITALIAN DRESSING

½ cup olive oil
¼ cup wine vinegar
1 clove garlic, pressed
½ tsp. oregano
salt, pepper

Blend dressing ingredients, pour on salad, and toss.

Cold Lemon Soufflé

Serves 8. 1-quart soufflé dish.

1 envelope plain gelatin
½ cup cold water
6 egg yolks
1 cup sugar
¾ cup lemon juice
1 Tbs. grated lemon rind
4 egg whites, beaten stiff
1½ cups heavy cream, whipped

Soften gelatin in cold water.

Beat yolks and sugar until light. Add lemon juice, and cook over low heat, stirring until thickened. Add gelatin, and stir until dissolved. Mix in rind. When custard is cool, fold in stiffly beaten whites and whipped cream. Pour into soufflé dish and chill.

FIRST DAY OF MAY BRUNCH

Rhine Wine Cooler

Spinach Soufflé Roll

English Muffin Loaf

Citrus Marmalade

Strawberries

Shortbread

Rhine Wine Cooler

One serving.

1½ tsp. sugar
1 Tbs. lemon juice
½ cup Rhine wine, chilled
crushed ice

Mix sugar with lemon juice until dissolved. Add wine. Pour over crushed ice in glass and garnish as suggested.

GARNISH

lemon slices, mint sprigs, or cucumber spears.

English Muffin Loaf

Yield: 2 loaves. Oven 400°F. Two 9-inch loaf pans, greased, and sprinkled with corn meal.

6 cups unsifted flour
2 packages yeast
1 Tbs. sugar
½ tsp. baking soda
2 tsp. salt
2 cups milk
¾ cup water
corn meal to sprinkle on pans

Combine 3 cups flour, yeast, sugar, soda, and salt. Heat milk and water to lukewarm. Add to yeast mixture. Beat well. Add remaining flour. Form loaves, and let rise in pans about 45 minutes. Bake for 25 minutes. Remove from pans, and cool on rack. This is good both warm from the oven and toasted.

Citrus Marmalade

Yield: 1 pint.

1 grapefruit
1 orange
3 quarts water

1 lemon, thinly sliced
1½ quarts water

4-6 cups sugar

Chop pulp of grapefruit and orange, and slice peel thinly. Boil peel for 5 minutes, in 1½ quarts water. Drain and repeat. To drained peel, add lemon, grapefruit, and orange pulp, and 1½ quarts water. Boil 5 minutes. Cover and let stand 12-18 hours. Bring to boil and cook rapidly 40 minutes until peel is tender. Add sugar. Bring to boil and stir until sugar dissolves. Cook to jelly stage — about 30 minutes — stirring often. Pour into hot sterilized jars and seal.

Spinach Soufflé Roll

Serves 8. Oven 400°F. Jelly-roll pan, greased, lined with wax paper, and greased again. Dust with flour.

ROLL

4 Tbs. butter
½ cup flour
2 cups milk
salt and pepper
5 eggs, separated

Melt butter, blend in flour, stir in milk and seasoning, and boil 1 minute. Beat yolks slightly, and add in slow stream to hot sauce, stirring. Do not allow to boil. Cool to room temperature, stirring occasionally. Beat whites until stiff, and fold into cooled sauce. Spread evenly in prepared pan. Bake 30 minutes until puffed and browned. Turn out onto clean towel.

HAM AND SPINACH FILLING

4 Tbs. minced onion
4 mushrooms, chopped
2 Tbs. butter
1 cup chopped cooked spinach
1 cup chopped or ground cooked ham
1 Tbs. Dijon mustard
¼ tsp. nutmeg
6 oz. cream cheese
salt and pepper

To prepare filling, sauté onion and mushrooms in butter for about 3 minutes. Add other ingredients, and stir together. Spread roll with filling, and roll up lengthwise. Place on a hot platter.

Strawberries

Serves 4-6.

½ cup fresh orange juice
1 Tbs. curaçao or to taste
1 quart fresh strawberries, sliced
1 cup whipped cream

Blend orange juice and curaçao. Pour over strawberries and refrigerate 2 hours or longer. Serve with whipped cream on the side.

Shortbread

Oven 300°F. Cookie sheet, or three 7-inch round tins.

½ lb. unsalted butter
½ cup superfine sugar
3 cups flour

Rub butter into flour and sugar until mixture resembles fine bread crumbs. Knead until butter is worked in completely.

Method 1. Roll out dough ½- to ¾-inch thick. Cut into triangles, place on cookie sheet, and prick with fork.
Method 2. Divide dough into 3 parts. Pat into round tins. Smooth, crimp edge, and score into 8 pieces.

Bake for 30 minutes, until shortbread is just beginning to change color. Cool before taking from tins.

MAY BASKET SUPPER

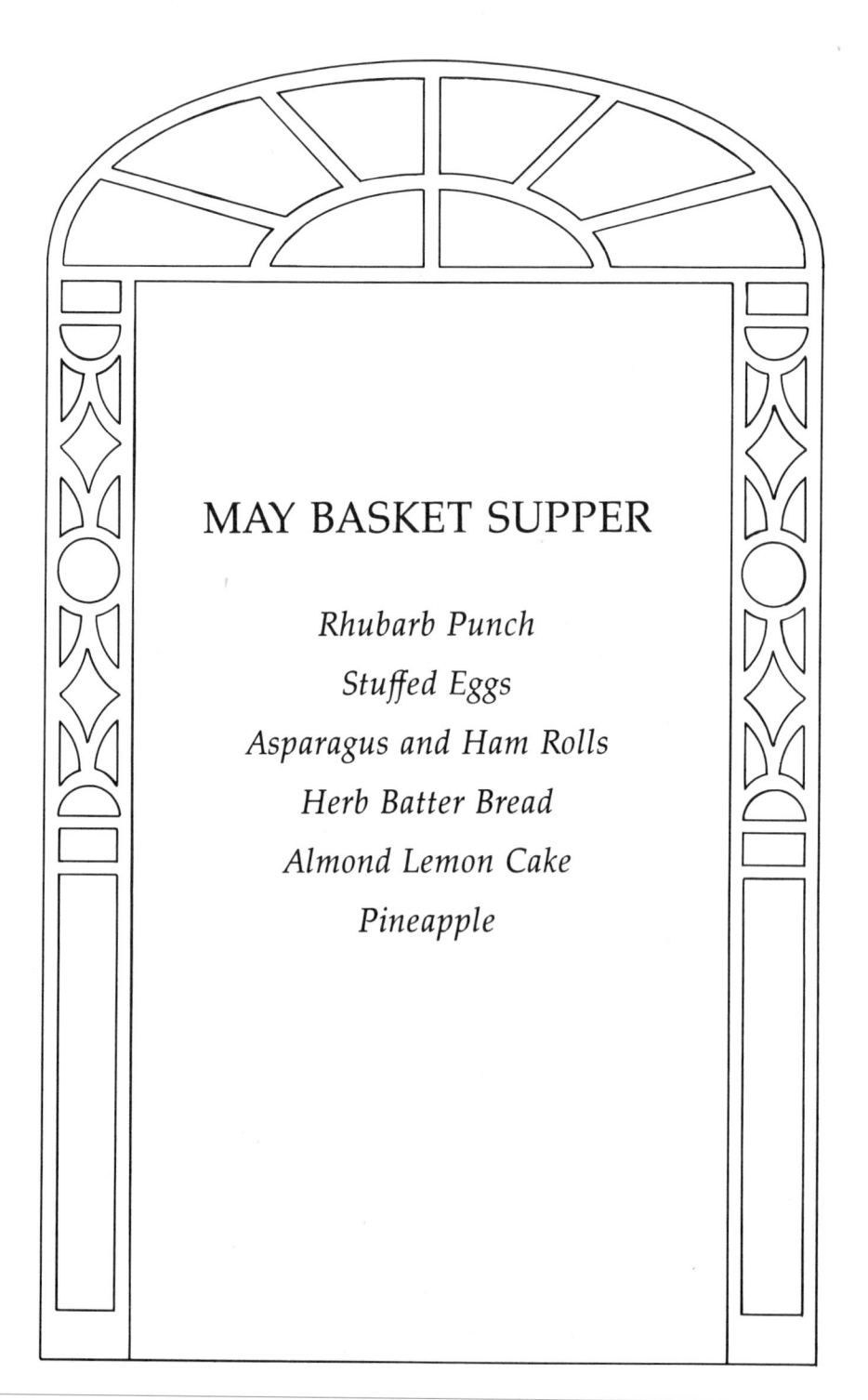

Rhubarb Punch

Stuffed Eggs

Asparagus and Ham Rolls

Herb Batter Bread

Almond Lemon Cake

Pineapple

Rhubarb Punch

Yield: 1 gallon — 25 punch cups.

5-6 stalks fresh rhubarb, or 3 cups cut up
2½ cups water
1 cup sugar
2 cups grapefruit juice
1 cup lemon juice
2 quarts gingerale

GARNISH
mint leaves
sliced lime

Cook rhubarb gently in water over low heat until mushy — about 15 minutes. Puree in blender. Add more water if necessary to make 4 cups. Stir in sugar until dissolved. Add other ingredients and chill. Serve over ice. Garnish as suggested.

Stuffed Eggs

Each variation serves 4.

CURRIED EGGS
4 hard-boiled eggs
salt, pepper to taste
1 tsp. curry powder
1-2 Tbs. mayonnaise
green pepper strips

Halve eggs, take out yolks, and mash together with other ingredients. Pipe mixture back into shells, and decorate with green pepper.

TOMATO EGGS
4 hard-boiled eggs
2 Tbs. catsup
¼ tsp. salt
¼ tsp. dry mustard
few drops Worcestershire sauce
⅛ tsp. cayenne pepper

Halve eggs, take out yolks, and mash together with other ingredients. Fill shells and decorate if desired.

Asparagus and Ham Rolls

Serves 4. Oven 325°F. Flat casserole, greased.

12 baked ham slices, medium thick
12 fresh asparagus spears, parboiled

Roll 1 asparagus spear (or 2 if thin) in each slice of ham. Place in casserole. Bake for 20 minutes.

Herb Batter Bread

Oven 375°F. 9-inch loaf pan, greased.

1 package yeast
1¼ cups warm water
2 Tbs. softened margarine
2 tsp. salt
2 Tbs. sugar
3 cups flour
½ tsp. nutmeg
1 tsp. powdered sage
2 tsp. caraway seeds

melted butter

In mixer bowl, dissolve yeast in warm water. Add margarine, salt, sugar, and ½ the flour. Beat 2 minutes. Add remaining flour and spices. Blend until smooth. Cover and let rise until double. Beat 25 strokes. Spread batter evenly in pan. Let rise until batter fills pan, about 45 minutes. Bake 45-50 minutes. Brush top of baked loaf with melted butter.

Almond Lemon Cake

Serves 20. Oven 325°F. 9-inch spring-form pan, greased, or 9-inch cake pan, greased, lined with wax paper, greased again.

CRUST

2⅔ cups flour
1⅓ cups sugar
1⅓ cups unsalted butter, or margarine
½ tsp. salt
1 egg

FILLING

1 cup ground almonds
½ cup sugar
1 tsp. grated lemon rind
1 egg, slightly beaten
½ tsp. almond extract

GARNISH

24 whole almonds

In large bowl, blend all crust ingredients until dough forms. Chill. Divide dough in half. Spread half on bottom of pan. Roll the other half between 2 sheets of wax paper into 9- or 10-inch circle.

Mix all filling ingredients. Spread over bottom crust to within ½ inch of sides of pan. Remove wax paper from top crust, and place top crust over filling. Press dough down over filling. Seal with fork. Decorate top with whole almonds. Bake 55-60 minutes. This is a *rich* cake. Serve thinly sliced.

MEMORIAL DAY LUNCH

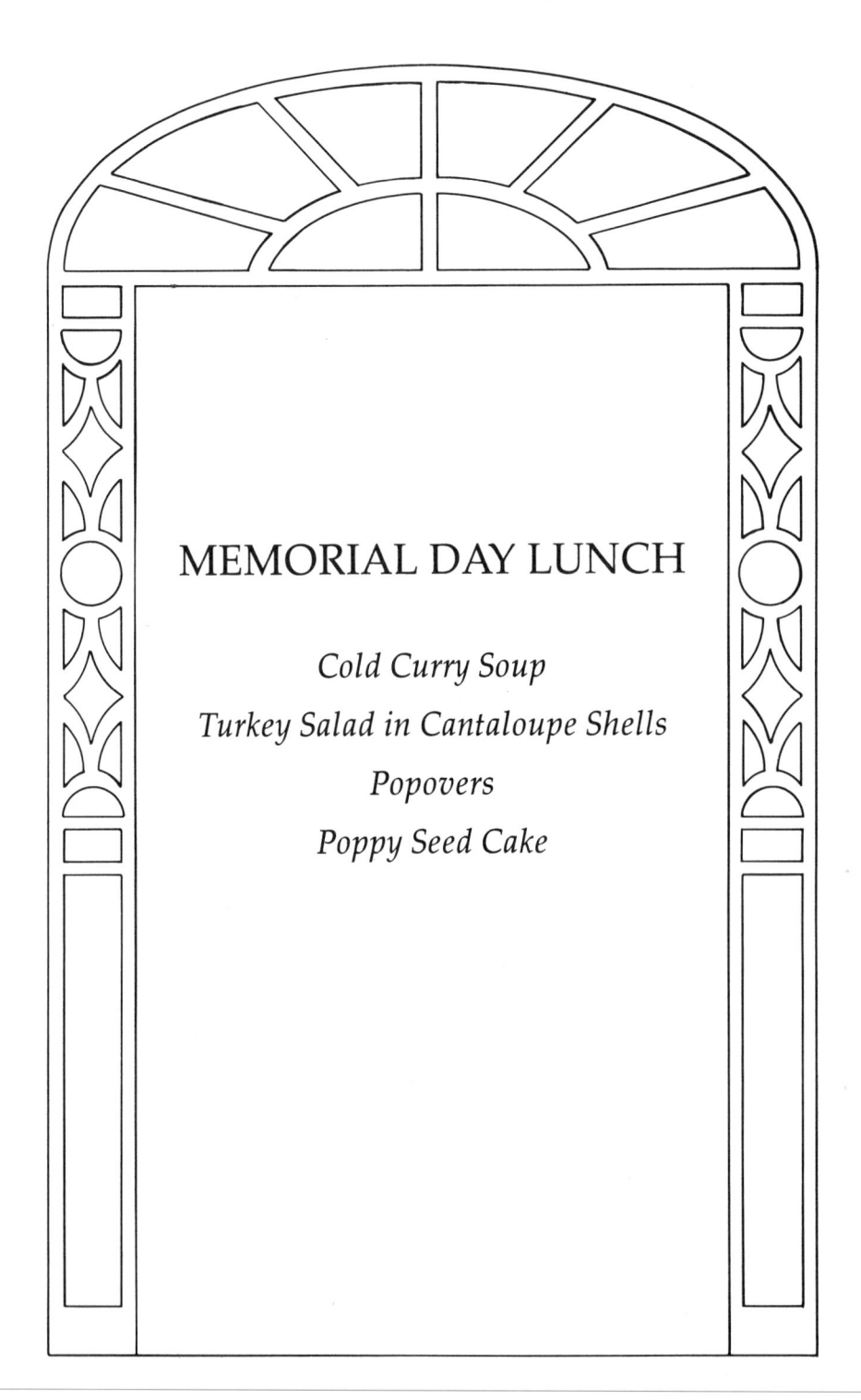

Cold Curry Soup

Turkey Salad in Cantaloupe Shells

Popovers

Poppy Seed Cake

Cold Curry Soup

Serves 8.

1 onion, chopped **1 carrot, diced** **½ stalk celery, chopped** **3 Tbs. margarine**	Sauté vegetables in margarine for 5 minutes.
2 Tbs. curry powder **1½ Tbs. flour** **1 Tbs. tomato paste** **3 cups chicken stock** **2 cups water**	Blend in curry powder and flour. Add tomato paste. Stir in liquids.
1 Tbs. almond paste **1 Tbs. red currant jelly** **10 whole cloves** **1 stick cinnamon** **1½ cups heavy cream** **2 Tbs. shredded coconut**	Add the next 4 ingredients, and simmer for ½ hour. Strain, cool, and refrigerate several hours or overnight. To serve, blend in heavy cream, and sprinkle coconut on top.

Turkey Salad in Cantaloupe Shells

Serves 4.

2 cups diced turkey meat **½ cup diced celery** **8-oz. can water chestnuts, drained and sliced** **¼ cup French oil-and-vinegar dressing**	Marinate first 3 ingredients in dressing 3 hours or overnight.
mayonnaise to taste **1 cup sliced green grapes** **½ cantaloupe shell per serving** **chutney**	Before serving add mayonnaise and grapes and spoon into cantaloupe shells. Garnish with chutney.

Popovers

Serves 6. Six glass custard cups, well buttered.

2 eggs lightly beaten with fork
1 cup milk
½ tsp. salt
1 Tbs. sugar
1 cup flour

To eggs, add milk, salt, and sugar, Stir lightly. Add flour, and mix only enough to moisten completely. Pour batter into cups, filling each cup ½ full. Place in *cold oven*. Turn heat to 425°F. and bake for 25 minutes. Turn down heat to 350°F. for 15 minutes more. Serve immediately, with lots of butter.

Poppy Seed Cake

Oven 350°F. 9-inch tube pan, greased and floured.

1 cup poppy seeds
¼ cup water
⅓ cup honey
1 cup butter
1½ cups sugar
4 eggs, separated
1 cup sour cream
1 tsp. vanilla

2½ cups sifted flour
1 tsp. baking soda
1 tsp. salt

confectioners' sugar

Combine poppy seeds, water, and honey. Cook over medium heat 5-7 minutes. Cool. Cream butter and sugar until light and fluffy. Stir in cooled poppy seed mixture. Add egg yolks one at a time, beating well after each addition. Stir in sour cream and vanilla. Sift together flour, soda, and salt. Gradually add dry ingredients to poppy seed mixture, beating well after each addition. Beat egg whites to soft peaks and fold into batter. Turn batter into prepared pan, and bake 1 hour and 15 minutes, or until cake springs back when lightly touched with finger. Cool in pan 5 minutes, then remove to rack. Before serving, dust with confectioners' sugar.

BUFFET SUPPER

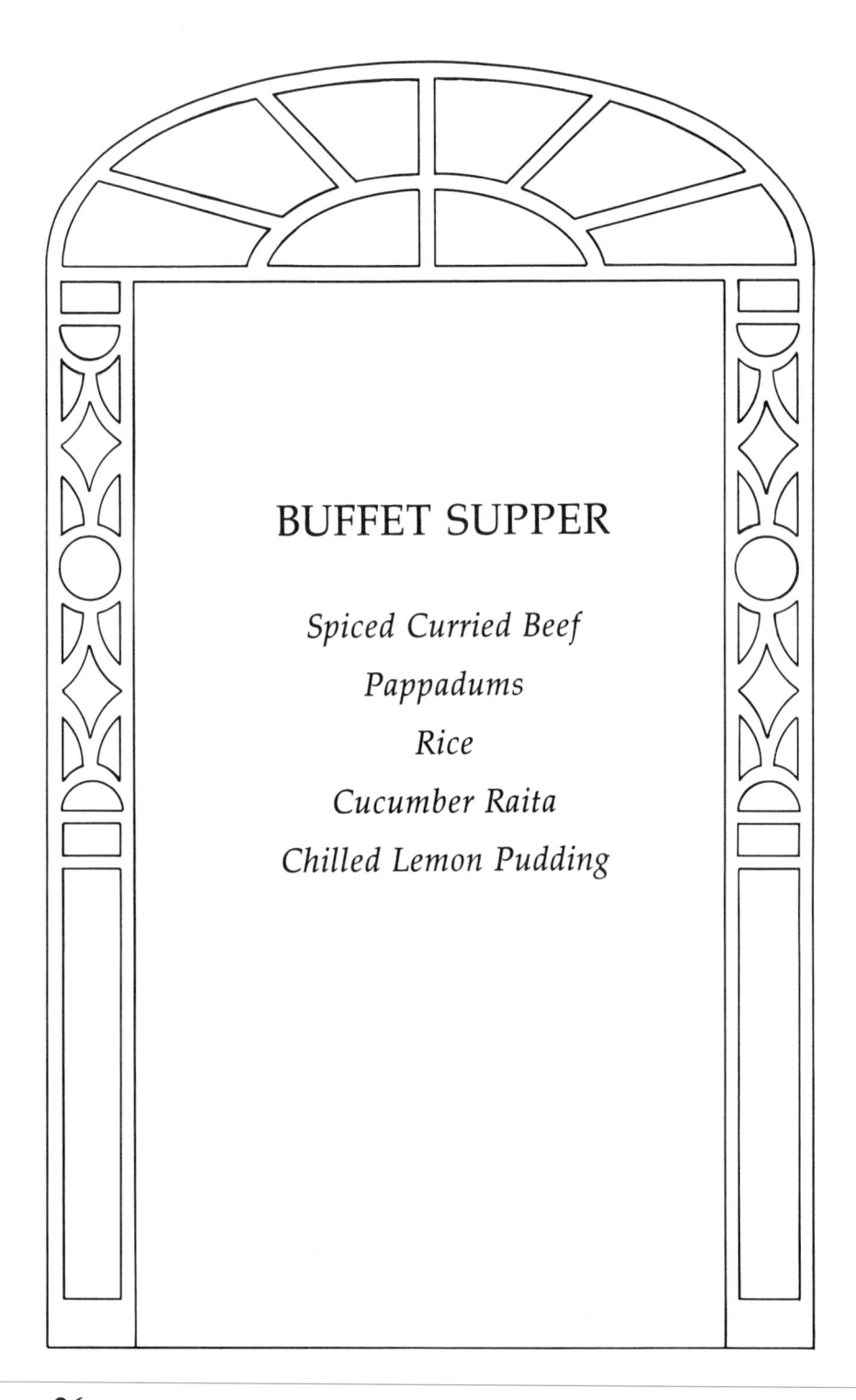

Spiced Curried Beef

Pappadums

Rice

Cucumber Raita

Chilled Lemon Pudding

Spiced Curried Beef

Serves 8-10.

- 3-4 medium onions, chopped
- 1 Tbs. olive oil
- 1 Tbs. margarine
- 4 lbs. beef, cut in 1-inch cubes
- 32-oz. can Italian tomatoes
- 2 tsp. salt
- ½ tsp. chili powder

- 4 Tbs. curry powder
- 2 Tbs. vinegar
- ½ Tbs. sugar
- rice

CONDIMENTS
raisins, coconut, chopped green peppers, chopped scallions, chutney, chopped hard-boiled eggs, chopped apple

Sauté onions in oil and margarine. Take from skillet and set aside. In same oil and margarine (adding more if necessary), brown meat. Drain tomatoes, but save juice. To browned meat, add tomatoes, onions, salt, and chili powder. Cover and simmer 30 minutes.

Blend curry with vinegar and sugar, and add. Cover and simmer for 2 hours. Add tomato juice if extra liquid needed. Serve over rice, with condiments on separate plates.

Pappadums

A traditional accompaniment to Indian curries, pappadums look like tortillas, but are made from lentil flour, peanut oil, and salt. They can be purchased at gourmet or health-food stores. To prepare, cook briefly in hot oil. They will puff up.

Cucumber Raita

Serves 6-8.

2 medium cucumbers

Seed cucumbers, and dice finely. Let stand an hour, then drain.

DRESSING

8 oz. yogurt
½ tsp. cumin seeds
½ tsp. salt

Mix dressing. Refrigerate one hour. Add cucumbers and garnish as suggested.

GARNISH

fresh coriander, or parsley sprigs

Chilled Lemon Pudding

Serves 8. 9 x 13-inch pan, greased.

2 cups crushed vanilla wafers
4 eggs, separated
1 cup sugar
3 Tbs. lemon juice
grated rind of one lemon
3 Tbs. plain gelatin dissolved in ½ cup hot water
1 cup heavy cream, whipped

Put 1 cup wafer crumbs in bottom of pan. In double boiler, cook egg yolks, ½ cup of sugar, lemon juice, and rind. Stir until custard coats spoon. Stir in gelatin mixture, and cool. Whip egg whites until stiff with remaining ½ cup sugar. Fold into custard. Fold in whipped cream. Sprinkle remaining crumbs on top. Chill until set. Overnight is best.

AFTER THE SPRING DANCE

Swiss Eggs

Sour Dough Streusel Coffee Cake

or

Sour Dough Date-Raisin Coffee Bread

Coffee Bar

Swiss Eggs

Oven 350°F. 8 ramekins, buttered.

1 lb. bacon strips **½ lb. Gruyère cheese, sliced** **8 eggs** **salt, pepper**	Cut bacon strips in half and fry crisp. Drain. Put a layer of cheese in ramekin bottoms. Lay crisp bacon strips over cheese. Break one egg, as you would for fried or poached, with yolk whole, into each ramekin over bacon. Season. Bake for 10-15 minutes or until eggs are set.

Sour Dough Streusel Coffee Cake

Serves 6-8. Oven 350°F. 8 x 12-inch pan, or bundt pan, greased.

2 cups flour
1 cup sugar
½ tsp. salt
2½ tsp. baking powder
2 eggs, beaten
¾ cup milk
½ cup vegetable oil
2 cups sour dough starter
  (see p. 6)
½ cup raisins
½ cup chopped nuts

Sift dry ingredients together; add liquids, starter, raisins, and nuts. Pour into baking pan.

TOPPING
1 cup brown sugar
2 Tbs. flour
2 tsp. cinnamon
¼ cup soft margarine

Mix topping ingredients. Sprinkle over top of batter, and bake for 50 minutes.

Sour Dough Date-Raisin Coffee Bread

Serves 6-8. Oven 400°F. Cookie sheet, or 12 x 8-inch pan, greased.

½ sour dough bread recipe (see p. 21)

FILLING
½ cup white raisins
½ cup chopped dates
½ cup chopped nuts
¾ cup brown sugar
1 tsp. cinnamon
½ tsp. ground cloves
1 cup margarine

soft margarine

Roll out dough on floured board into 12 x 8-inch oblong. Combine filling ingredients, and spread over dough oblong. Roll up dough lengthwise over filling, and seal edges to prevent dough from sliding. Place on baking sheet or pan to rise for 1 hour. Bake on bottom rack of preheated oven for 30 minutes or until loaf sounds hollow when tapped on top, and is a nice brown. Brush top with soft margarine while still hot.

Coffee Bar

coffee, cinnamon sticks, lemon peel, whipped cream, assorted liqueurs

PORCH SUPPER

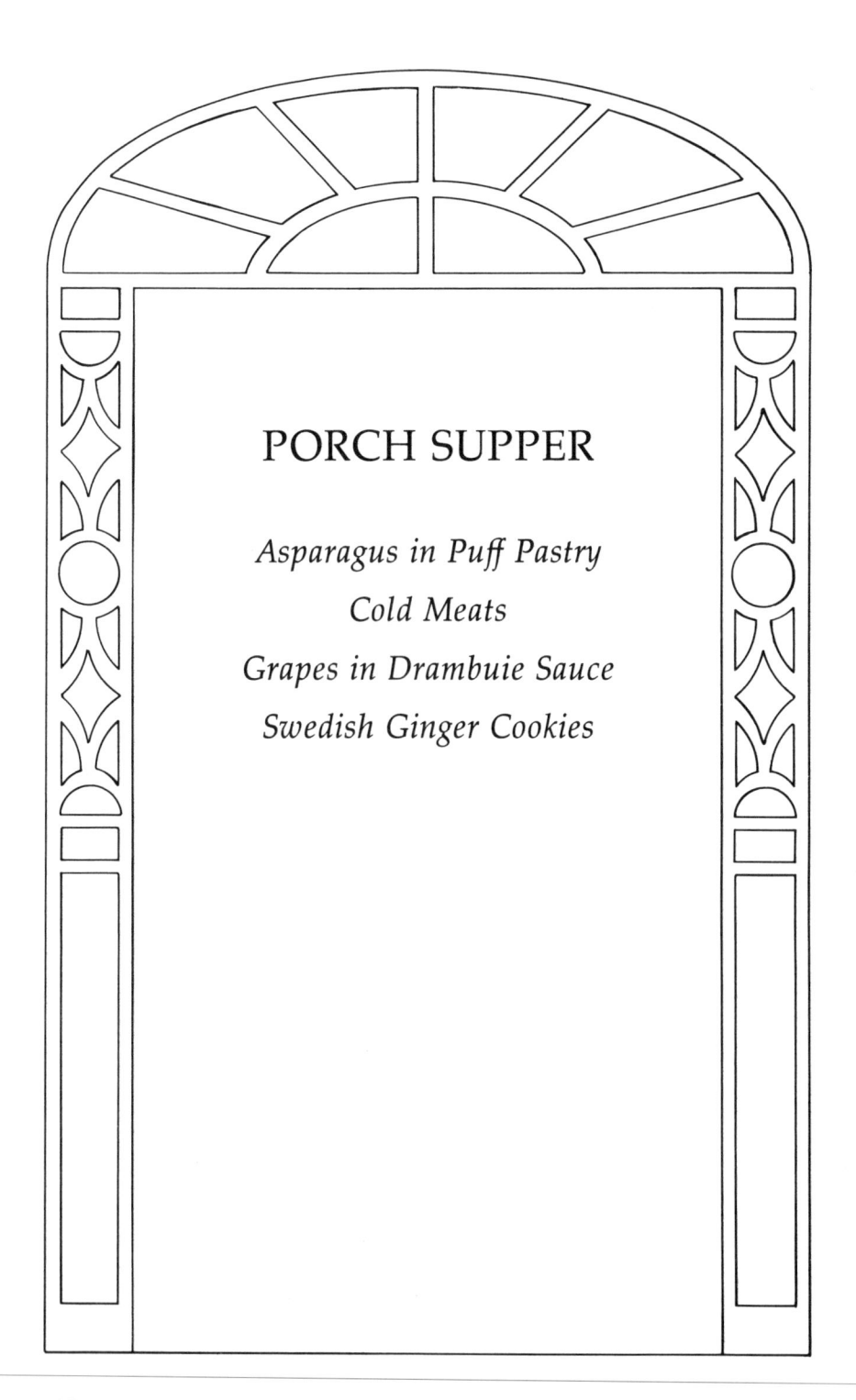

Asparagus in Puff Pastry
Cold Meats
Grapes in Drambuie Sauce
Swedish Ginger Cookies

Asparagus in Puff Pastry

Serves 6.

puff pastry for 6
1 bunch fresh asparagus, trimmed and cooked
¼ lb. butter
juice of 2 lemons

Bake pastry and split. Place asparagus spears lengthwise on bottom of split pastry, and cover with top half of pastry. Melt butter, whisk in lemon juice, and spoon over filled pastries. Serve hot.

Grapes in Drambuie Sauce

Serves 6.

1 cup yogurt, or sour cream
⅓ cup honey
3 Tbs. Drambuie
2 tsp. lemon juice
1½ lbs. seedless green grapes

Mix first 4 ingredients.

Toss with grapes, and chill.

Swedish Ginger Cookies

Oven 375°F. Cookie sheets, ungreased.

1 cup butter
1½ cups sugar
1 egg
1½ Tbs. grated orange peel
2 Tbs. dark corn syrup
1 Tbs. water
3¼ cups sifted flour
2 tsp. baking soda
2 tsp. cinnamon
1 tsp. ginger
½ tsp. cloves
blanched almond halves

Cream butter and sugar. Add egg. Beat until fluffy. Add peel, corn syrup, and water. Sift dry ingredients together, and add. Chill dough. Roll ⅛ inch thick. Cut into diamonds or desired shapes. Decorate with almond halves. Place cookies 1 inch apart on pan. Bake 8-10 minutes. Remove from pan and cool on rack.

Summer

SUMMER BRUNCH

Spritzer

Leeks with Ham in Dill Sauce

Brioche

Strawberry Rhubarb Mold

Corn-Meal Butter Cookies

Spritzer

equal parts: white wine and soda water

Serve over ice.

Leeks with Ham in Dill Sauce

Serves 6.

12 leeks, ¾-inch to 1-inch thick, with 1-inch green stems
12 slices prosciutto, or Virginia ham
2 eggs
2 tsp. Dijon mustard
1-2 tsp. white wine vinegar
salt and pepper
2-3 Tbs. chopped fresh dill, or ½ tsp. dried
1 cup peanut oil
2 Tbs. chopped green onions

Simmer leeks in water 10-15 minutes. Drain. Wrap each leek in ham slice. Mix eggs and remaining ingredients except onions in blender, adding oil slowly. Add onions to sauce. Place leeks on serving platter, and cover with sauce. Serve chilled, or at room temperature.

GARNISH

chopped fresh parsley

Garnish as suggested.

47

Brioche

Oven 425°F. Muffin tins.

1 package yeast
½ cup lukewarm water
4 cups flour
1 tsp. salt
1 Tbs. sugar
¾ cup softened butter
6 eggs

egg yolk, beaten

Dissolve yeast in water. Stir in 1 cup flour. Let rise 1 hour, covered. Mix remaining flour with salt, sugar, butter, and 3 eggs. Beat well in mixer. Beat in remaining eggs, and add yeast mixture. Let rise in greased bowl for 3 hours. Beat dough, then chill overnight. Roll dough in palms to make balls, each filling a muffin cup ½ full. Cut an "X" in top of each ball. Make smaller balls and insert into each "X." Cover, and let rise in warm place until double; about 1 hour. Brush tops with beaten egg yolk. Bake for 20 minutes. Serve hot.

Strawberry Rhubarb Mold

Serves 8. 2-quart mold.

3 cups diced rhubarb
½ cup sugar
¼ cup water
6-oz. package strawberry gelatin
¾ cup cold water
1 cup finely chopped celery
¼ cup lemon juice
1 cup sliced strawberries

Simmer rhubarb and sugar in ¼ cup water until rhubarb is soft. Add gelatin and stir until dissolved.

Add remaining ingredients. Chill until firm.

Corn-Meal Butter Cookies

Yield: 50 cookies. Oven 350°F. Cookie sheets, ungreased.

½ lb. unsalted butter
1 cup sugar
2 egg yolks
1 tsp. grated lemon peel
1½ cups flour
1 cup yellow corn meal

Cream butter and sugar until light. Add yolks, lemon peel, flour, and corn meal. Chill dough until firm. Roll into long cylinder. Cut into ¼-inch slices, or roll out and cut into shapes. Bake 10-12 minutes.

CANOEING ON THE CONCORD RIVER

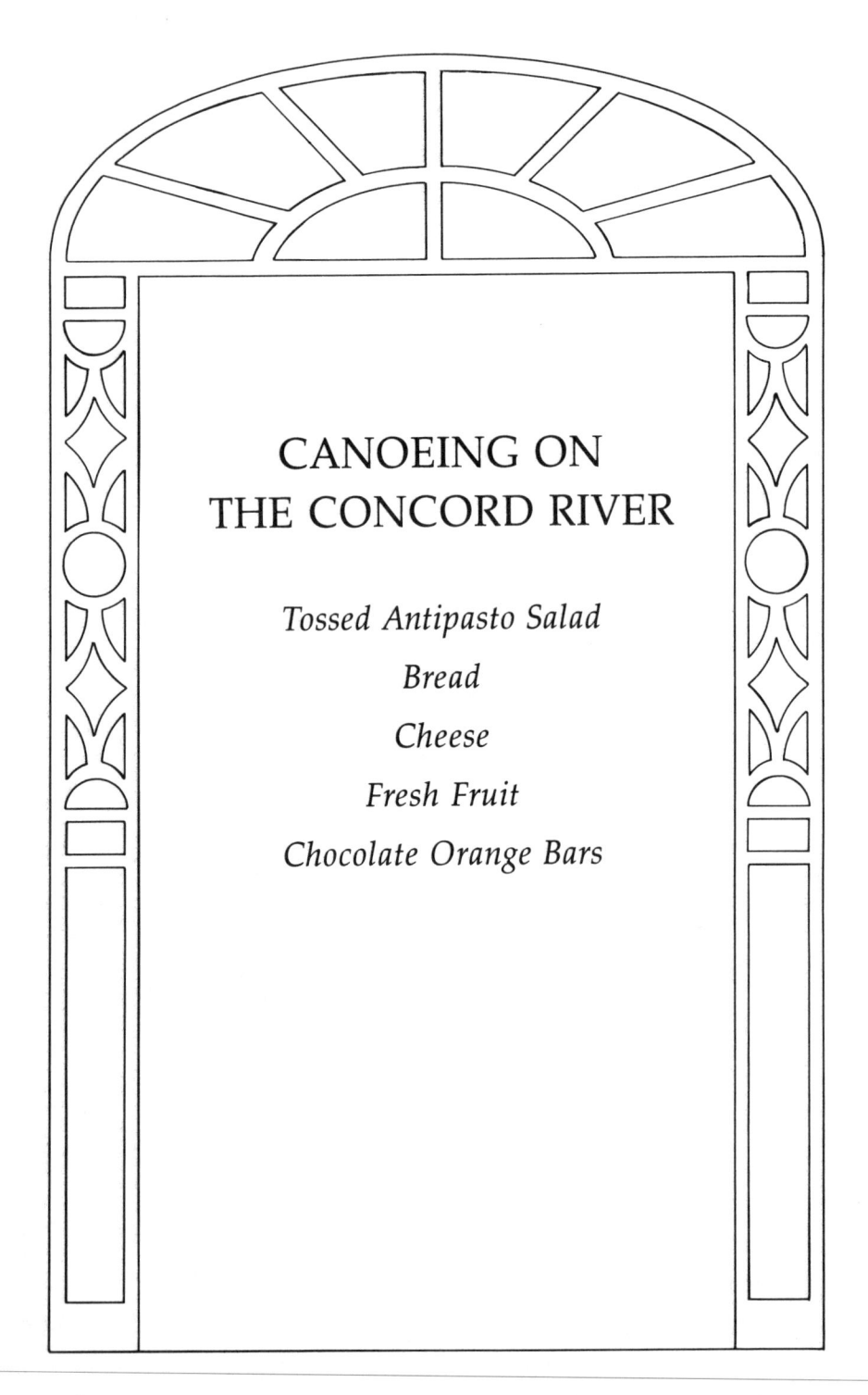

Tossed Antipasto Salad

Bread

Cheese

Fresh Fruit

Chocolate Orange Bars

Tossed Antipasto Salad

Serves 6-8.

3 carrots, scraped, and cut julienne
3 stalks celery, cut into ½-inch pieces
2 cups cauliflower flowerets
1 green pepper, cut in strips
1 cup fresh mushroom caps
1 can black olives, drained
8½-oz. can artichoke hearts, drained and halved
½ cup wine vinegar
¼ cup olive oil
1-2 Tbs. sugar, to taste
1 tsp. salt
½ tsp. oregano
¼ tsp. freshly ground pepper
¼ cup water

Mix all ingredients in saucepan, and bring to boil. Simmer 5 minutes. Cool, and chill overnight.

GARNISH

cherry tomatoes, basil, and parsley

Garnish as suggested, and serve with bread, cheese, and fruit of your choice.

Chocolate Orange Bars

Oven 350°F. Jelly-roll pan, greased.

1¼ cups flour
½ tsp. salt
¾ tsp. baking soda
¾ cup brown sugar
½ cup water
½ cup butter
1¼ cups chopped dates
6 oz. chocolate bits
2 eggs, beaten
½ cup orange juice
½ cup milk
1 cup chopped walnuts

Sift flour, salt, and soda. Heat brown sugar, water, butter, and dates, until dates soften. Cool. Add chocolate and eggs. Stir well. Add dry ingredients alternately with juice and milk. Stir in nuts. Bake 25-30 minutes.

ORANGE GLAZE FROSTING

1½ cups confectioners' sugar
2 Tbs. soft butter
1 Tbs. grated orange or lemon rind
½ tsp. orange or lemon extract
2-3 Tbs. cream

Blend frosting ingredients until smooth. Frost bars when cool.

FOURTH OF JULY

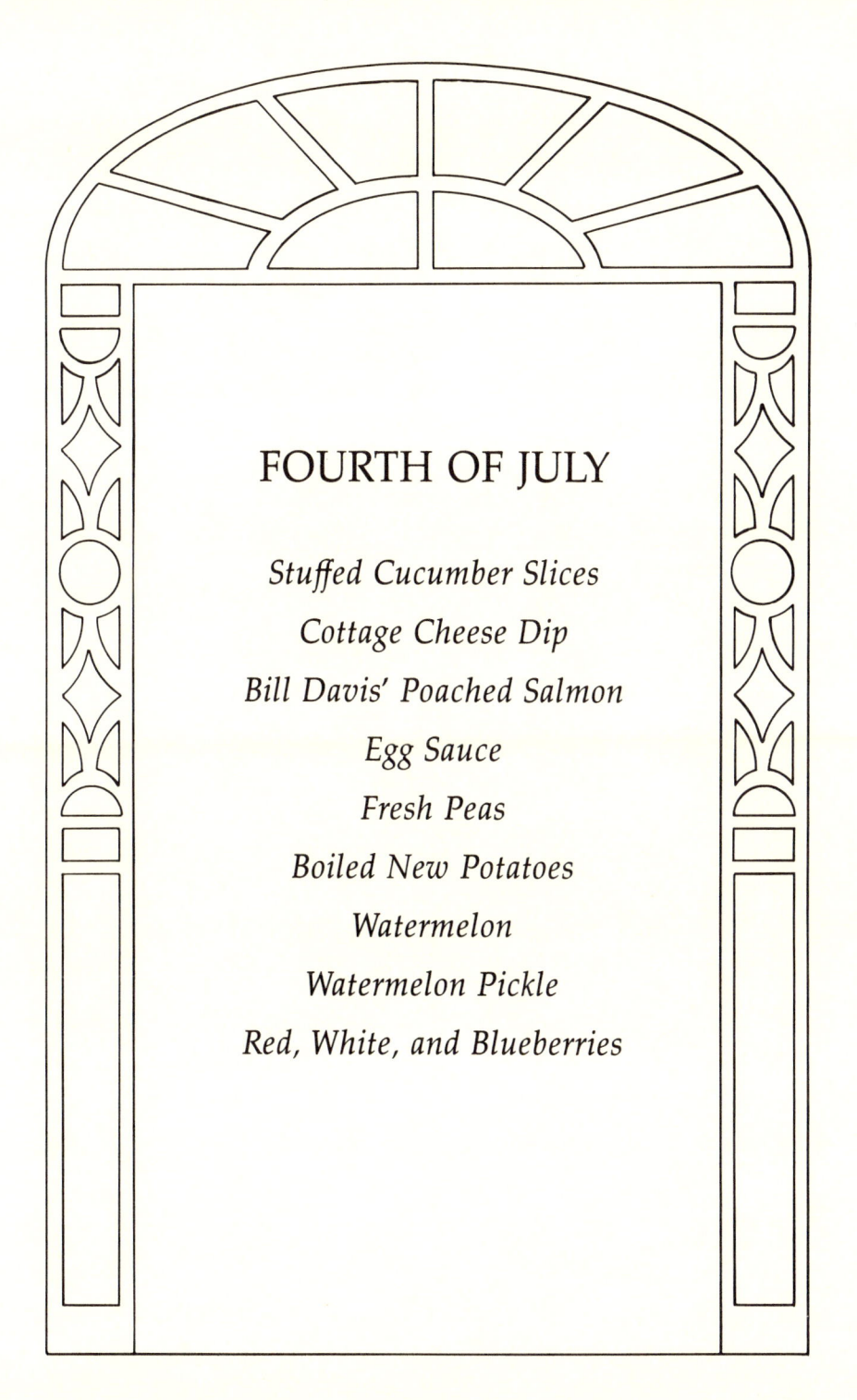

Stuffed Cucumber Slices
Cottage Cheese Dip
Bill Davis' Poached Salmon
Egg Sauce
Fresh Peas
Boiled New Potatoes
Watermelon
Watermelon Pickle
Red, White, and Blueberries

Stuffed Cucumber Slices

Yield: 2 dozen.

3 cucumbers
2 Tbs. minced onion
1 cup cream cheese, whipped
3-oz. jar red caviar

Cut cucumbers in half lengthwise. Remove seeds. Mix onion with cream cheese. Stuff cucumbers. Top with caviar. Cut into 1-inch slices.

Cottage Cheese Dip

3 cups cottage cheese
½ cup mayonnaise
1 Tbs. lemon juice
sour cream
1 carrot, grated
3 scallions, chopped
1 green pepper, chopped
2 stalks celery, chopped
pepper to taste
fresh herbs as desired

Combine cottage cheese, mayonnaise, and lemon juice. Add sour cream to make desired consistency. Mix in vegetables and herbs. Chill.

1 tomato, skinned, seeded, and chopped

Just before serving add tomato. Serve with crackers.

Bill Davis' Poached Salmon

Serves 8.

COURT BOUILLON

2 cups water
1½ cups dry white wine
2 small onions, sliced
2 stalks celery, chopped
2 or 3 carrots, chopped
1½ tsp. salt
1 bay leaf
8 peppercorns

Combine court bouillon ingredients. Bring to boil and simmer 30 minutes.

SALMON

eight 4-oz. salmon steaks

Add fish, cover pan, and simmer 5 minutes, or until salmon flakes. Lift steaks out with pancake turner to hot platter. Keep hot while you make egg sauce.

EGG SAUCE

3 Tbs. melted butter
3 Tbs. flour
fish stock, reduced to 1½ cups
1 cup light cream
2 hard-boiled eggs, sieved
1 Tbs. chopped fresh dill
¼ tsp. white pepper

Blend butter and flour over low heat. Add fish stock, stirring until smooth and thickened. Blend in cream. Stir in eggs, dill, and pepper. Pour over salmon steaks and serve.

Watermelon Pickle

Yield: 5 quarts.

rind of 1 large watermelon

alum water: to each quart of water allow 2 tsp. powdered alum.

Cut away all green outside skin from watermelon rind, and any remaining pink fruit. Cut into small bite-sized cubes. Prepare enough alum water to cover cubes. Boil in alum water until transparent, and pieces can be easily pierced with a fork. Do not overcook. Drain.

SYRUP

7 cups white sugar
3 cups white vinegar
4 sticks cinnamon
1 Tbs. whole cloves
1 Tbs. cassia buds
½ Tbs. whole allspice

Mix syrup ingredients. Bring to boil and pour over cooked rind. Let stand overnight. Next morning, drain off syrup, bring syrup to boil again, and pour over rind. Repeat this process for 3 successive days. Drain and pack into hot sterile jars. Boil syrup again and fill jars to overflowing. Seal immediately and store in cool place.

Red, White, and Blueberries

Serves 8.

½ cup water
½ cup sugar
1½ cups fresh blueberries, or unsweetened frozen
1½ Tbs. cornstarch
1½ Tbs. water
½ tsp. vanilla
1 Tbs. lemon juice

In small saucepan, bring water and sugar to boil. Add blueberries, bring to boil, and simmer 2 minutes. Skim fruit from liquid with slotted spoon and set aside. Blend cornstarch and water to make smooth paste, and stir into blueberry liquid. Cook, stirring, until thick, clear, and bubbling. Remove from heat and add vanilla and lemon juice. Let cool slightly, then return blueberries to sauce. Chill covered.

2 cups whole strawberries
vanilla ice cream

Gently mix in strawberries. Serve over vanilla ice cream.

CONCORD BAND CONCERT PICNIC SUPPER

Cold Zucchini Soup

Brandade Fish Salad

Syrian Bread

Marinated Green Beans

Cheese Cake with Strawberries

The outdoor concerts played by the Concord Band are joyous summer occasions. These take place on the lovely grounds of the North Bridge Visitors Center overlooking the Concord River. The Band presents a varied menu of Sousa favorites, symphonic arrangements, current show tunes, and Dixieland. Family members, from tiny babies to great aunts, come with their blankets and picnic hampers. The most enthusiastic participants are the young children inspired to strut, pirouette, and "conduct."

Cold Zucchini Soup

Serves 8.

- 2 large onions, chopped
- 1 clove garlic, minced
- 2 Tbs. margarine
- 2 lbs. zucchini, sliced
- 4 cups chicken stock (homemade for best flavor)
- 1½ Tbs. wine vinegar
- ½ tsp. salt
- ¼ tsp. pepper
- 2 potatoes, sliced

GARNISH
yogurt, or sour cream

Sauté onions and garlic in margarine until soft. Place all ingredients in saucepan, bring to boil, and simmer 30 minutes. Cool. Puree soup in blender in small amounts. Chill overnight.

Serve cold, garnished as suggested.

Brandade Fish Salad

Serves 8.

- 2 lbs. white fish — cod, haddock, or flounder
- 2 Tbs. lemon juice
- 10 peppercorns
- 4 slices white bread
- ¼ cup olive oil
- 4 cloves garlic, crushed
- salt and pepper
- mayonnaise

GARNISH
sliced gherkins, capers

Poach fish in boiling water with lemon juice and peppercorns. Cool in broth. Drain, skin, and bone. Remove crusts from bread, and soak in a little water with 1 Tbs. olive oil. Squeeze dry. With wooden spoon, work fish into bread. Add oil gradually with garlic and a few drops of lemon juice. Salt and pepper to taste. Stir in enough mayonnaise to get good consistency. Chill. Garnish as suggested.

Syrian Bread

Yield: 12 mini loaves, or 6-8 sandwich size. Oven 500°F. Cookie sheet, ungreased.

1 tsp. honey **2 Tbs. yeast** **2 cups lukewarm water** **¼ cup soy flour** **2 tsp. salt** **¼ cup wheat germ** **4-6 cups flour, white and whole wheat, combined**	In large bowl, stir honey with yeast in ½ cup lukewarm water. Set aside about 10 minutes or until mixture starts to foam. Add soy flour, salt, wheat germ, and rest of water (1½ cups). Add flours, until dough is tacky.

Turn out on board and knead for 10 minutes, using additional flour as needed. Dough will be a bit tacky and very elastic. Put dough into greased bowl, turning to grease all sides. Cover and let rise until double, about 1½ hours. Punch down and turn out on board. Cut into desired sizes and form each into a ball. Leave these out for 30 minutes covered. Roll balls out to about ¼ or ⅛ inch thick. They must be well floured on both sides. They will not puff if they stick to cookie sheet. Place on *ungreased* cookie sheet, and let rise uncovered for another 20-30 minutes, no more. Bake for 6 to 10 minutes, or until light brown and puffy. Remove from oven, place on board, and cover with towel. As bread cools, steam will escape, and loaves will flatten, leaving pocket under top crust. Towel keeps loaves from drying out while steam escapes.

Marinated Green Beans

Serves 4-6.

- 1 lb. fresh green beans
- ⅓ cup olive oil
- 1 Tbs. lemon juice
- 1 tsp. salt
- ⅛ tsp. pepper
- ¼ cup chopped onion
- 1 Tbs. fresh dill

Steam beans in ½ inch boiling water. Drain. Combine other ingredients. Pour over hot beans. Chill. Serve on lettuce with tomato wedges and hard-boiled egg slices.

Cheese Cake

Serves 8. Oven 350°F. 10-inch pie plate.

CRUST
- 1½ cups graham cracker crumbs
- ½ cup confectioners' sugar
- 1 tsp. allspice
- ⅓ cup melted margarine

Add margarine to dry ingredients. Press crust into bottom of pan.

FILLING
- two 8-oz. packages cream cheese
- 2 eggs, beaten
- ⅔ cup sugar
- 2 tsp. vanilla

Beat cheese until soft, then mix in other ingredients. Pour into pan over crust. Bake for 25 minutes.

TOPPING
- 1½ cups sour cream
- 4 Tbs. sugar
- 2 tsp. vanilla

Pour topping on hot pie, and return to oven for 7 minutes at 450°F. Cool and chill.

GARNISH
- fresh strawberries

Serve with strawberries.

RAINY DAY SUPPER

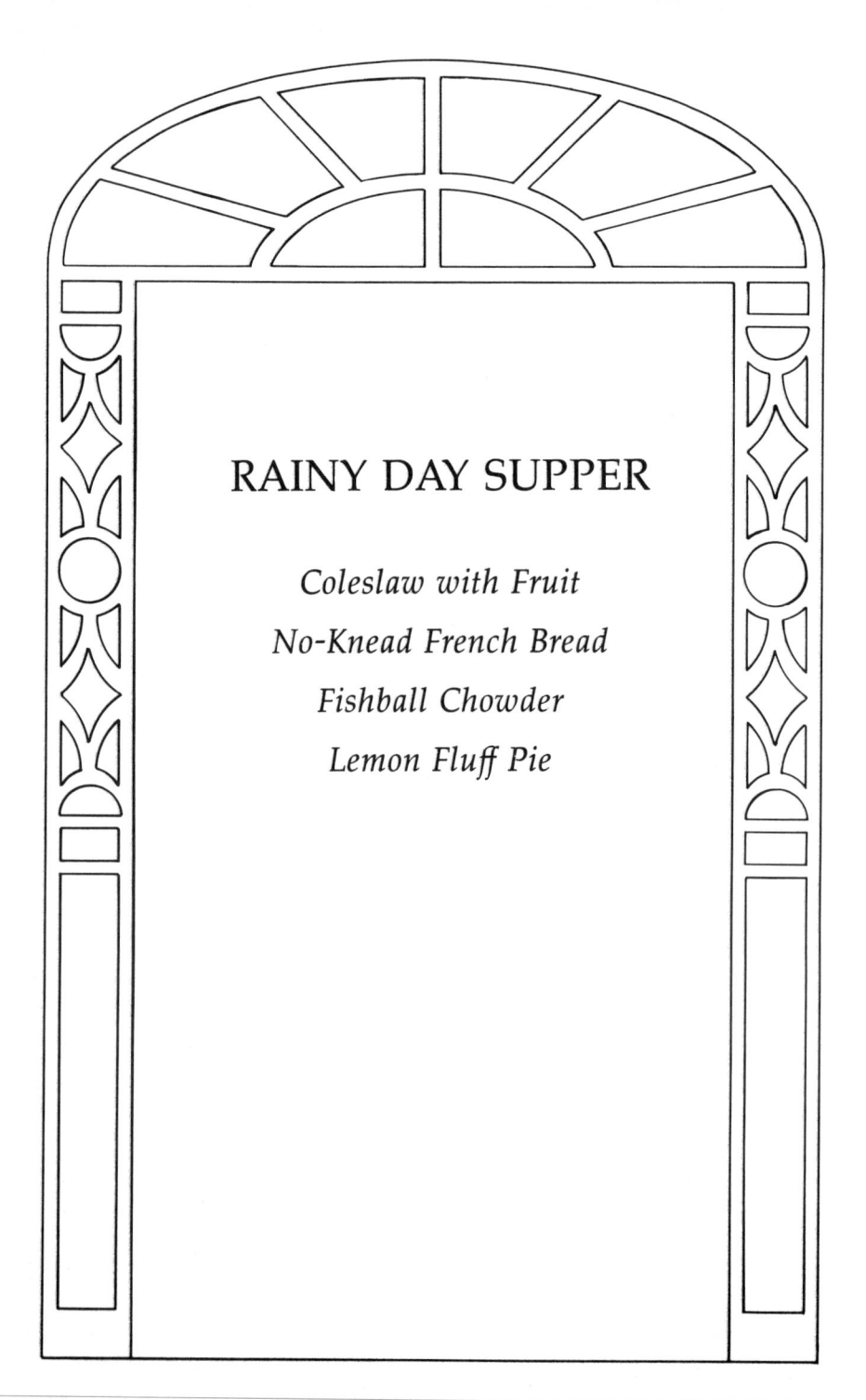

Coleslaw with Fruit

No-Knead French Bread

Fishball Chowder

Lemon Fluff Pie

Coleslaw with Fruit

Serves 8.

4 cups shredded purple and green cabbage 1 cup diced apples 1 cup sliced grapes (red or purple for color) 1 carrot, shredded 2 Tbs. lemon juice 1½ tsp. salt	Toss all together and chill.
1 cup sour cream 1 Tbs. honey 2 tsp. crushed fennel seeds	Combine and serve on coleslaw.

No-Knead French Bread

Oven 400°F. Cookie sheet, sprinkled with corn meal.

1 package yeast 2 cups lukewarm water 4-5 cups unbleached flour 1 Tbs. sugar 1 tsp. salt **egg yolk, beaten** **sesame seeds**	Dissolve yeast in ½ cup lukewarm water. Add 1 cup flour. Then stir in remaining 1½ cups lukewarm water, sugar, and salt. Stir in remaining flour. Let dough rise until double. Punch down, and let rise again. Punch down, shape loaf, brush with beaten yolk, and sprinkle with sesame seeds. Bake 40 minutes or until done.

Fishball Chowder

Serves 8.

CHOWDER

- 4-5 lb. whole haddock
- 4 cups water — to cover fish parts
- 1 large carrot, sliced
- 2 stalks celery, sliced
- 2 onions, sliced
- 3 sprigs parsley
- 3 bay leaves
- 1 tsp. tarragon
- 1 tsp. dill
- 4 cups cubed potatoes (6 medium)
- 1 quart milk
- 1 tsp. salt
- ¼ tsp. white pepper
- pinch cayenne
- 3 Tbs. butter

FISHBALLS

- haddock fillets
- ¼ cup crushed chowder crackers
- 1 tsp. salt
- ½ tsp. white pepper
- 2 Tbs. melted butter
- 2 eggs, well beaten
- dill, tarragon, and parsley to taste

Have fish filleted. Reserve fillets. Place head, tail, and bones in kettle with water to cover. Add vegetables (except potatoes) and seasonings. Simmer ½ hour. Strain and reserve broth.

Cook potatoes in reserved broth until just soft. Scald milk in double boiler. Add potatoes to milk with salt, pepper, cayenne, and butter. Save the fish broth to cook the fishballs.

Grind reserved fish fillets, or chop very fine. Mix other ingredients with fish, and shape into 1-inch balls. Cook a few at a time in boiling broth for 4-5 minutes. Remove with slotted spoon as they rise to top and are white. Handle gently. Add fishballs to hot milk mixture.

(continued)

½ lb. salt pork, diced into tiny cubes

Try out salt pork slowly in skillet until golden. Drain pork bits, and reserve. Sprinkle over chowder at serving time. Best if made a day ahead. Fishballs can be frozen.

Lemon Fluff Pie

Serves 6. 9-inch pie plate.

9-inch baked pie shell
4 large eggs, separated
1 cup sugar
juice and grated rind of 1 lemon
1 envelope plain gelatin, softened in 2 Tbs. water
1 oz. unsweetened chocolate
1 Tbs. butter

In saucepan, beat yolks. Add ½ cup sugar, juice, and rind. Stir over low heat until thick. Add softened gelatin and stir until dissolved. Cool slightly. Beat whites until stiff and beat in remaining ½ cup sugar. Fold into custard. Melt chocolate and butter. Spread on pie shell before filling with lemon mixture. Chill. Sets in 2 hours.

SUMMER REUNION LUNCHEON

Cold Potato Soup

Soused Fish

Whole Wheat Refrigerator Rolls

Spinach, Lettuce, and Chopped Egg Salad

Gertrude Fallon's Sour Cream Dessert

Cold Potato Soup

Serves 6.

3 large potatoes, peeled, quartered
1 large stalk celery, chopped
½ cup chopped celery leaves
1 medium onion, chopped
2 tsp. chopped fresh dill
1½ cups chicken stock
½ cup milk

Cook vegetables with dill in 1 cup chicken stock until tender. Whirl in blender until smooth. Return to saucepan with remaining ½ cup stock and milk. Add more stock and/or milk if necessary. Cool, then chill for several hours. Also good served hot.

GARNISH

2 Tbs. chopped chives

Garnish as suggested.

Soused Fish

Serves 6.

4 oz. wine vinegar
10 oz. dry white wine
10 oz. water
1 onion, thinly sliced
2 bay leaves
2 tsp. salt
6 peppercorns
1 tsp. brown sugar
6 herring, mackerel, or trout fillets
tomato slices

Bring all ingredients except fish to boil, and simmer 15 minutes. Add fish, cover, and simmer 10 minutes. Remove from heat, and cool fish in pan. Chill.

Serve with tomato slices.

Whole Wheat Refrigerator Rolls

Yield: 12 rolls. Oven 375°F.

1¼ cups lukewarm water or potato water
½ cup sugar
1 tsp. salt
1 package yeast
¼ cup lukewarm water
2 eggs, beaten
⅔ cup soft shortening
1 cup mashed potato
3 cups white flour
3 cups whole wheat flour
toasted wheat germ

Combine 1¼ cups lukewarm water, sugar, and salt. Dissolve yeast in ¼ cup lukewarm water. Add to first mixture, along with eggs, shortening, and potato. Stir in flours. Knead, using wheat germ instead of flour on board. (Adds flavor and texture.) Place dough in greased bowl, turning to grease all sides, and cover with wax paper, a damp towel, and plastic wrap. Store up to 5 days in refrigerator. If dough rises, punch down, and return to refrigerator. Form into rolls as needed, and let rise in a warm place for at least 2 hours. Bake for 25 minutes. This dough is also good for sweet buns, or may be shaped into 2 bread loaves.

Spinach, Lettuce, and Chopped Egg Salad

Serves 4-6.

spinach leaves, Bibb lettuce
3 hard-boiled eggs, chopped

Wash and crisp greens, then tear into bite-sized pieces and toss with eggs.

PAPRIKA DRESSING

1 cup oil
1 tsp. paprika
¼ cup white vinegar
1 tsp. salt
1 tsp. minced onion
1 tsp. dry mustard

Combine dressing ingredients and blend well. Just before serving, pour over salad, and toss.

Gertrude Fallon's Sour Cream Dessert

Serves 6.

½ pint cream, whipped
½ cup sour cream
½ cup yogurt
brown sugar

blueberries

Fold whipped cream into sour cream and yogurt. Place in serving bowl. Sprinkle top *thickly* with brown sugar. Chill. This dish is best made the day before, so the top can melt and form a crust. Serve with blueberries.

COOL LIGHT SUPPER

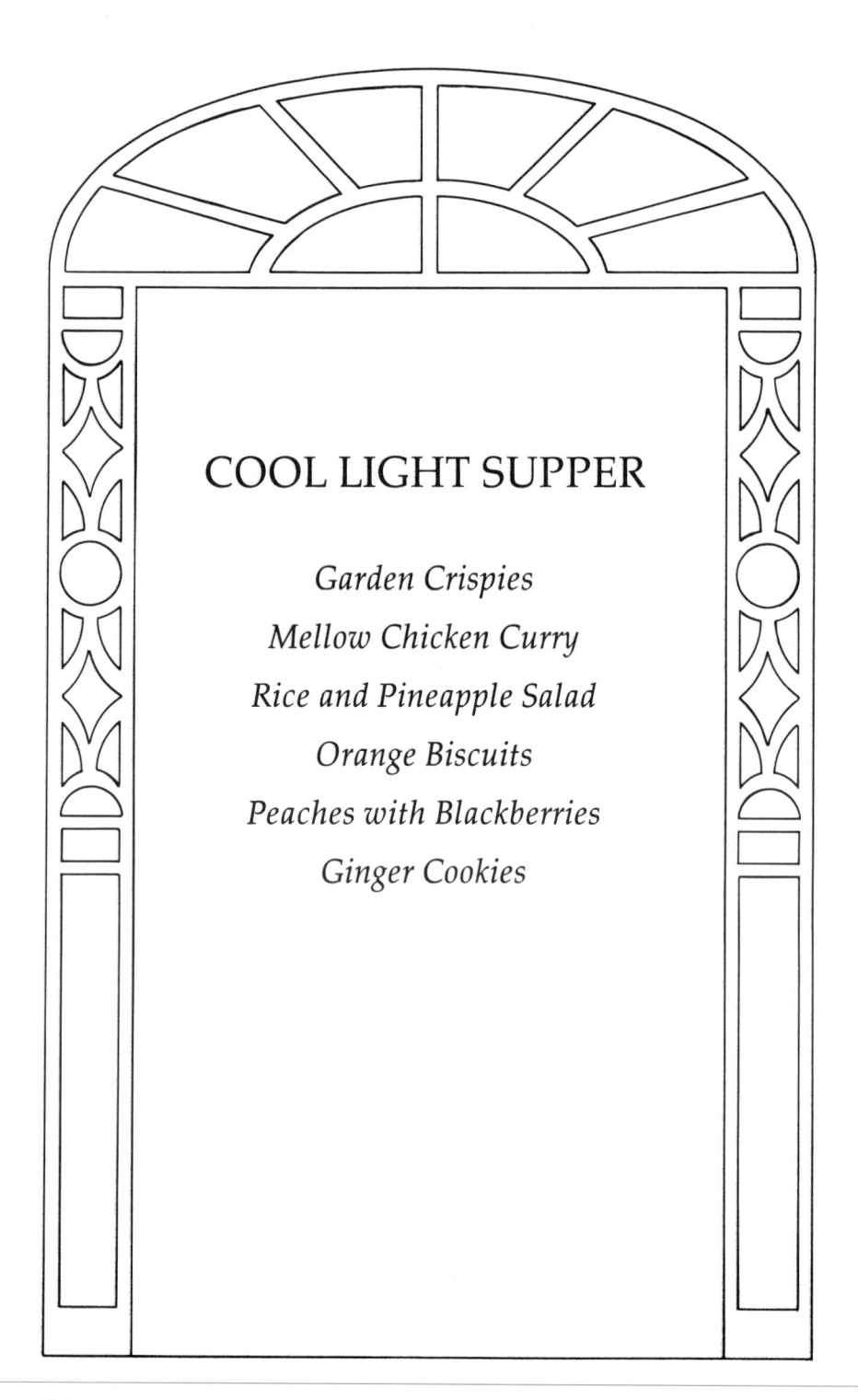

Garden Crispies

Mellow Chicken Curry

Rice and Pineapple Salad

Orange Biscuits

Peaches with Blackberries

Ginger Cookies

Garden Crispies

crisp apple, green or yellow, sliced across
cream cheese, softened
cucumber slices
radish slices

Spread apple rounds with cream cheese, top with cucumber, spread again with cheese, and top with radish.

GARNISH

sprigs of basil, mint, or parsley

Garnish as suggested.

Mellow Chicken Curry

Serves 6.

CURRY MAYONNAISE

1 small onion, chopped
1 Tbs. oil
1 Tbs. curry powder
⅔ cup chicken stock
1 Tbs. tomato paste
2 Tbs. sweet chutney
2 Tbs. lemon juice
1 cup mayonnaise
2 Tbs. cream

Sauté onion in oil for 5 minutes. Stir in curry powder. Add stock, tomato paste, chutney, and lemon juice. Bring to boil and simmer 5 minutes. Strain and cool. Stir in mayonnaise and cream.

4-lb. chicken, roasted, cooled

Slice chicken meat, and cover with mayonnaise.
Place in refrigerator for several hours for flavors to meld.

Rice and Pineapple Salad

Serves 6.

¾ cups long-grain rice
4 Tbs. oil and vinegar dressing
2 slices fresh or canned pineapple, chopped
1 small green pepper, chopped
4 scallions, chopped
2 Tbs. raisins
lettuce

Cook rice in boiling water *al dente* 8-10 minutes. Drain. Stir in 2 Tbs. dressing to glaze rice kernels. Cool. Mix in all other ingredients with remaining 2 Tbs. dressing. Allow flavors to blend for several hours. Serve on lettuce.

Orange Biscuits

Yield: 1 dozen. Oven 425°F. Cookie sheet, greased.

2 cups flour
½ tsp. salt
4 tsp. baking powder
¼ cup shortening
¾ cup milk
sugar cubes
orange juice

Sift dry ingredients. Cut shortening into mixture to consistency of coarse meal. Add milk all at once. Mix. Turn dough onto a floured board to form a ball — handle as little as possible. Pat into circle ½ inch thick. Cut into 2-inch rounds. Place a sugar cube dipped in orange juice deeply into the middle of each biscuit. Moisten hole slightly with a little more orange juice. Bake for 15 minutes.

Peaches with Blackberries

Select ripe fruits. Slice peaches, and mix with berries in serving bowl.

Ginger Cookies

Yield: 2 dozen. Oven 375°F. Cookie sheet, greased.

¾ stick butter
½ cup sugar
1 egg, beaten
1 cup flour
⅛ tsp. salt
1 tsp. baking powder
½ tsp. ground ginger
2 Tbs. chopped preserved ginger
2 cups cornflake crumbs

Cream butter and sugar. Add egg. Mix in all ingredients, except crumbs. Stir to blend. Drop small teaspoonfuls into cornflakes, and coat well. Bake for 20 minutes.

ICE CREAM SOCIAL

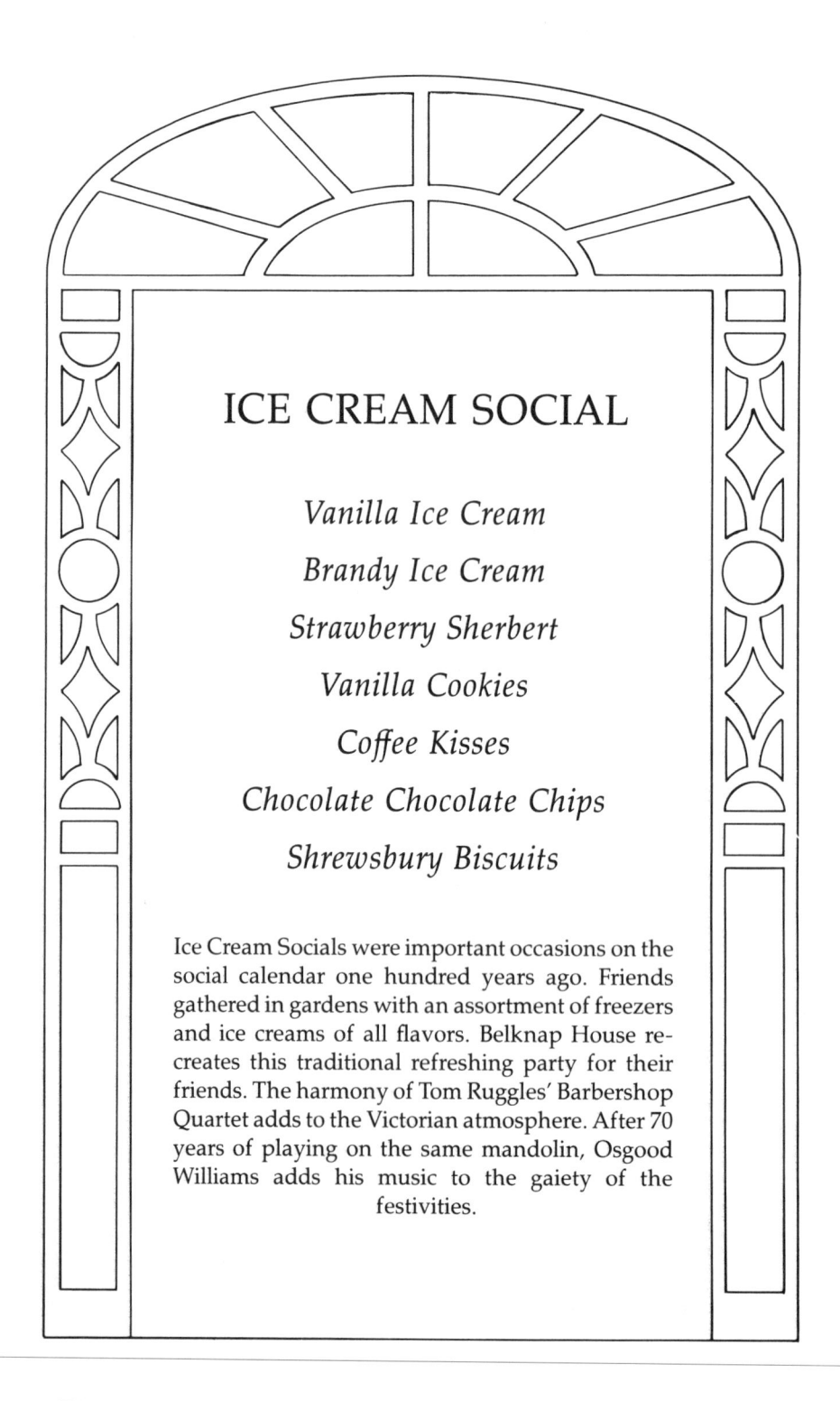

Vanilla Ice Cream

Brandy Ice Cream

Strawberry Sherbert

Vanilla Cookies

Coffee Kisses

Chocolate Chocolate Chips

Shrewsbury Biscuits

Ice Cream Socials were important occasions on the social calendar one hundred years ago. Friends gathered in gardens with an assortment of freezers and ice creams of all flavors. Belknap House re-creates this traditional refreshing party for their friends. The harmony of Tom Ruggles' Barbershop Quartet adds to the Victorian atmosphere. After 70 years of playing on the same mandolin, Osgood Williams adds his music to the gaiety of the festivities.

Vanilla Ice Cream

Yield: 1½ quarts. Old-fashioned hand-crank freezer.

1 quart thin cream
¾ cup sugar
⅛ tsp. salt
1¾ tsp. vanilla

Heat half the cream with sugar and salt, stirring until dissolved. Cool. Add remaining cream and vanilla. Chill in freezer can until ready to freeze. The can should not be more than ¾ full.

TO FREEZE:

10-20 pounds ice, shaved (if using cubes, they must be pounded)
rock salt — not table salt

Mix ice and salt in proportions of 1 part salt to 5 parts ice. Place freezer can in freezer. Add ice/salt around can, being sure drain hole is open.

Crank slowly at first, then faster. Cranking will become harder — let the little ones crank first. When it is very hard to turn put some weight on top — little ones can sit on it. Pour off some ice water and remove can. Pack down ice cream and let crankers lick the dasher. Cover can tightly with plastic wrap and return to freezer. Repack with ice/salt and cover freezer with an old blanket. The ice cream should be allowed to ripen for an hour to improve its texture.

Note: Because this ice cream has no emulsifiers it does not keep well in the home freezer — ice crystals will form.

Brandy Ice Cream

8-inch square pan.

4 eggs, separated
3 Tbs. brandy or rum
½ cup sugar
1½ cups heavy cream

Beat egg yolks with brandy and half the sugar. Beat whites with remaining sugar and fold together. Whip cream and fold in. Freeze 24 hours.

Strawberry Sherbert

9-inch square pan. 6-cup mold or bowl.

1 quart fresh strawberries
1 cup sugar (or less)
1½ pints plain yogurt

Wash and hull berries. Mix with sugar in blender or food processor. Blend in yogurt. Freeze in pan until firm (about 3 hours). Beat in chilled bowl until smooth. Spoon into mold or bowl, cover with foil or plastic, and freeze about 6 hours, or overnight.

Vanilla Cookies

Yield: Fifty 2-inch cookies. Oven 375°F. Cookie sheet, greased.

¼ lb. butter
1 cup sugar
½ tsp. vanilla
1 egg
2 cups flour
1 tsp. baking powder
½ cup raisins

Cream butter and sugar. Add other ingredients. Mix well. Roll dough into walnut-size balls. Place on cookie sheet and flatten with fork. Bake for 15-20 minutes.

Coffee Kisses

Yield: 50 cookies. Oven 275°F. Cookie sheet, greased.

2 egg whites
⅛ tsp. cream of tartar
1 tsp. white vinegar
½ tsp. salt
1¼ cups sugar
2 Tbs. instant coffee
1 tsp. vanilla
½ cup finely chopped nuts

Beat whites until frothy. Add cream of tartar, vinegar, salt, sugar, and coffee gradually while beating. Continue beating until stiff peaks are formed. Fold in vanilla and nuts. Drop by small spoonfuls onto baking sheet. Bake for 20-25 minutes.

Chocolate Chocolate Chips

Yield: about 50. Oven 350°F. Cookie sheet, greased.

⅓ cup cocoa
2 cups flour
½ tsp. baking soda
½ lb. butter
1 cup granulated sugar
½ cup dark brown sugar
1 tsp. vanilla
2 Tbs. milk
1 cup chopped pecans
1 cup semisweet chocolate bits

Sift dry ingredients together. Cream butter, sugars, and vanilla. Stir in dry ingredients alternately with milk. Add nuts and chocolate bits. Drop on cookie sheet by teaspoons. Bake for 12 minutes.

Shrewsbury Biscuits

Oven 350°F. Cookie sheet, greased.

¼ lb. butter
1 cup sugar
1 egg
1 Tbs. grated lemon rind
2 cups flour
1 tsp. baking powder
raspberry jam

Cream butter and sugar. Add egg and rind, and beat well. Add flour and baking powder. Knead, roll out, and cut into 2-inch rounds. Make a small hole in center of every other biscuit. Bake 15-20 minutes. Cool, and when cold, put biscuits with holes and whole rounds together with jam.

NEIGHBORHOOD COOKOUT

Shandy

Cucumber Dip

Herring and Macaroni Salad

Marinated Chuck Roast

Tomato Slices

Buttermilk Dressing

Blueberry Muffins

Tritical Bread

Pineapple-Mint Fantasy

Shandy

equal amounts light beer and lemonade

Mix beer and lemonade together; serve well chilled.

Cucumber Dip

2 cups yogurt
2 small cloves garlic, pressed
3 Tbs. olive oil
1 Tbs. chopped dill
2 tsp. chopped mint
salt and pepper
2 medium cucumbers, chopped

Before adding cucumbers, beat together all other ingredients. Chill for a few hours. Will keep for 2 weeks in refrigerator.

Herring and Macaroni Salad

Serves 4-6.

½ cup uncooked macaroni
½ cup chopped, cooked chicken or ham
6-8 pieces pickled herring, cut up

Cook macaroni as directed on package. Rinse in cold water. Drain and cool. Put meat and herring in bowl with macaroni.

DRESSING
4 Tbs. mayonnaise
1 Tbs. curry powder
2 Tbs. sour cream
½ tsp. salt
¼ tsp. white pepper

Prepare dressing. Toss with salad. Serve on lettuce.

lettuce

Marinated Chuck Roast

Serves 6-8.

3-5 lbs. chuck or London-broil steak
½ cup strong coffee
½ cup soy sauce
1 Tbs. Worcestershire sauce
1 Tbs. vinegar
1 Tbs. sesame seeds, browned in butter
1 large onion, chopped

Combine all ingredients. Let meat stand in marinade all day, or overnight. Turn it every few hours. Barbecue or broil.

Buttermilk Dressing

Serves 6-8.

1 cup mayonnaise
1 cup buttermilk
1 Tbs. marjoram
1 Tbs. chopped basil
1 tsp. powdered garlic
½ tsp. powdered onion
2 tsp. brown sugar

Mix well and chill. Serve on sliced tomatoes.

Blueberry Muffins

Yield: 1½ dozen. Oven 375°F. Muffin tins, greased.

¼ lb. butter 1¼ cups sugar 2 eggs 2 cups flour 2 tsp. baking powder ½ tsp. salt ½ cup milk 2 cups blueberries grated rind of 1 lemon	Cream butter and sugar until fluffy. Beat in eggs one at a time. Sift dry ingredients together. Add to creamed mixture alternately with milk. Carefully fold in blueberries and lemon rind. Fill muffin tins ⅔ full. Bake for 25-30 minutes.

Tritical Bread

Yield: 2 loaves. Oven 375°F. Two 9-inch loaf pans, greased.

1 Tbs. yeast 2 cups warm water 1 Tbs. molasses or brown sugar 1 tsp. salt 2 Tbs. safflower oil (or other vegetable oil) ½ cup whole wheat kernels 4 cups flour, half whole wheat and half white	Dissolve yeast in warm water. Add molasses, salt, oil, and wheat kernels. Stir in flours. Let dough rise in bowl for 1 hour or until double. Divide dough into pans. Dough will be sticky. Bake immediately for 45-50 minutes. Remove from pans, and cool on rack. For tender crust, brush hot loaves with butter. Store in refrigerator.

Pineapple-Mint Fantasy

Serves 12 or more. Oven 400°F. 8x12-inch pan.

COOKIE CRUST

1 cup flour
¼ cup brown sugar
½ cup margarine
½ cup chopped walnuts

Mix and press into pan to cover thinly. Bake 12-15 minutes. Cool.

FILLING

20-oz. can crushed pineapple, drained
3-oz. package lime gelatin
1 cup sugar
8 oz. cream cheese
⅔ cup evaporated milk, chilled and whipped
⅛ tsp. peppermint extract

Drain pineapple juice into saucepan. Heat and stir in gelatin to dissolve. Mix sugar and cheese, then add to gelatin. Cool. Add pineapple, whipped evaporated milk, and peppermint. Pour over baked, cooled crust and refrigerate.

GLAZE

½ cup semisweet chocolate morsels
⅓ cup evaporated milk
1 Tbs. butter
¼ tsp. peppermint extract

Melt chocolate over water. Add other ingredients. Stir and cool. Spread over pineapple filling. Chill overnight.

UNDER THE ARBOR AFTERNOON TEA

Eleanor Fenn's Iced Tea

Graham Cracker Praline Cookies

Zucchini Drop Cookies

Low-Sodium Raisin Cookies

Eleanor Fenn's Iced Tea

Yield: 8-10 cups.

VERSION I

2 Tbs. tea leaves
2 lemons, chopped or ground
2 cups sugar
2 Tbs. finely chopped mint leaves
2 quarts boiling water

Pour boiling water over other ingredients. Let stand for 5 or 10 minutes. Decant, and chill. This is Eleanor's original nineteenth-century recipe. It is *very* sweet.

VERSION II

2 quarts boiling water
8 or more sprigs mint
8 tea bags
1½ cups sugar
lemon juice to taste

Pour boiling water over mint and tea and steep 5 minutes. Remove tea and mint (squeeze out into pot). Add sugar and lemon juice. Stir until dissolved. Add ½ gallon ice. When ice is melted, strain tea into a gallon jug. Fill with cold water.

GARNISH

cinnamon sticks
mint sprigs

Garnish as suggested.

Graham Cracker Praline Cookies

Oven 350°F. Jelly-roll pan.

- 24 graham cracker squares, cut in halves (48 pieces in all)
- ¼ lb. butter
- ¼ lb. margarine
- ½ cup brown sugar
- 1 tsp. vanilla
- ½ cup chopped nuts

Lay out crackers on pan. Melt shortenings and sugar in saucepan. Boil for 2 minutes. Add vanilla and nuts. Spread evenly over crackers. Bake for 8 to 10 minutes, or until the whole surface is bubbling and brown. Remove from pan immediately.

Zucchini Drop Cookies

Oven 375°F. Cookie sheet, greased.

- 1 cup grated zucchini
- 1 tsp. baking soda
- 1 cup sugar
- ½ cup plus 3 Tbs. margarine
- 1 egg, beaten
- 2 cups flour
- 1 tsp. cinnamon
- ½ tsp. ground cloves
- (½ tsp. mace)
- ½ tsp. salt
- 1 cup chopped nuts
- 1 cup raisins
- 2 Tbs. yogurt

Mix and drop by teaspoonfuls onto cookie sheet. Bake for 12 to 15 minutes.

Low-Sodium Raisin Cookies

Yield: 4 dozen. Oven 350°F. Cookie sheets, greased.

½ cup unsalted butter
¾ cup white sugar
2 Tbs. brown sugar
1 egg
¾ cup raisins
½ cup walnuts
¾ cup flour
1 tsp. cinnamon
½ tsp. nutmeg
¼ tsp. allspice
1 cup oatmeal

Cream butter and sugars. Add egg. Chop raisins and nuts. Sift flour with spices. Mix in raisins and nuts and add to batter. Add oatmeal. Stir well. Drop by teaspoonfuls onto cookie sheet and flatten. They do not spread. Bake for 10 to 15 minutes. Do not overbake.

OUT OF THE GARDEN SUPPER

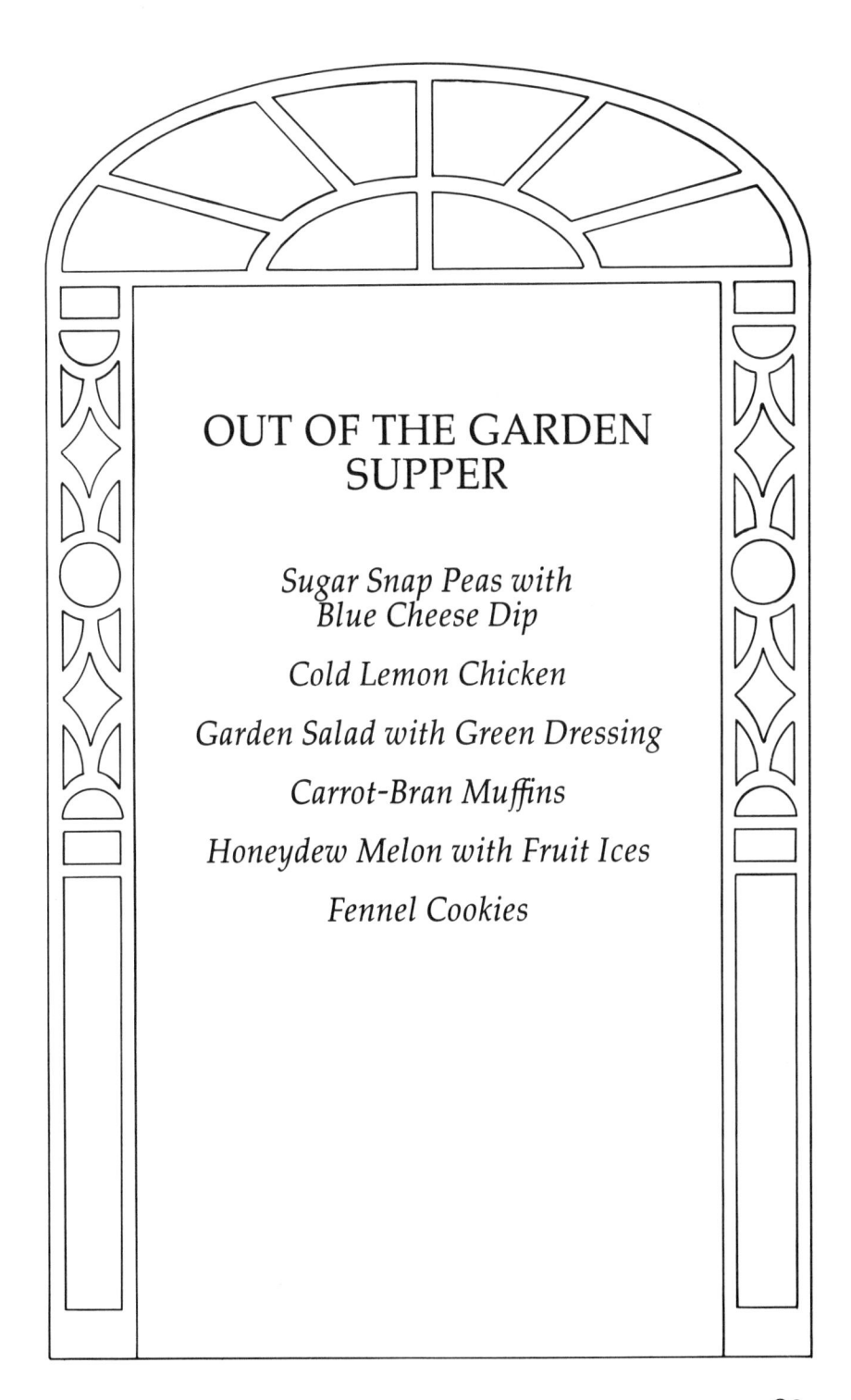

*Sugar Snap Peas with
Blue Cheese Dip*

Cold Lemon Chicken

Garden Salad with Green Dressing

Carrot-Bran Muffins

Honeydew Melon with Fruit Ices

Fennel Cookies

Sugar Snap Peas with Blue Cheese Dip

½ cup blue cheese
½ cup cream cheese
¼ cup mayonnaise
sugar-snap or snow pea pods (peas in)

Combine the cheeses with enough mayonnaise to make the right consistency. Stuff young sugar-snap or snow pea pods with mixture, using pastry tube. Be careful to not overstuff, or pods will split.

Cold Lemon Chicken

Serves 4-6.

4-lb. chicken, cut up
1 onion, sliced
1 bay leaf

Simmer chicken 1 hour in water with onion and bay leaf. Cool in broth. Remove bay leaf. Slice meat. Chill. Reserve broth.

SAUCE

2 Tbs. butter
1 Tbs. flour
1 cup chicken broth
2 egg yolks, beaten
1 cup cream
juice and rind of ½ lemon
salt and pepper

Melt butter, stir in flour, and cook gently 1 minute. Add broth slowly, and bring to boil, stirring, to make a smooth sauce. Simmer a few minutes. Add a little hot broth to egg yolks, stir, and return to saucepan to thicken sauce. Add cream, lemon juice, rind, salt, and pepper. Do not allow to boil. Pour over sliced chicken, and chill. Serve with rice if desired.

Garden Salad with Green Dressing

Yield: 1 pint dressing.

DRESSING

15 sprigs parsley
15 sprigs watercress
½ cup herb vinegar
½ cup olive oil
½ cup peanut oil
1 egg yolk
1 tsp. dry mustard
1 tsp. fresh tarragon
2 Tbs. chopped onion
½ tsp. salt
freshly ground black pepper

Place all ingredients in a blender or food processor, and blend until well homogenized.

Serve on a combination of greens fresh from the garden, perhaps including nasturtium flowers and leaves.

Carrot-Bran Muffins

Yield: 12 large muffins. Oven 375°F. Muffin tins, greased.

1 cup 40% bran flakes
2 cups finely grated carrots
¾ cup skim milk
2 Tbs. brown sugar
1 Tbs. lemon juice
½ tsp. baking soda
½ tsp. salt
1 cup whole wheat flour
2 Tbs. vegetable oil
1 tsp. baking powder
¼-½ tsp. cinnamon
1 egg, slightly beaten

Combine bran, carrots, and milk. Let stand 5 minutes.

Add all other ingredients, stirring until just moist. Fill muffin tins ½ full. Bake for 20 minutes. Muffins are done when top springs back when touched.

Honeydew Melon with Fruit Ices

Serves 4-6.

CANTALOUPE ICE

⅓ cup sugar
½ cup water
3½ cups pureed cantaloupe
juice of 1 lemon or lime

Bring sugar and water to boil, and dissolve sugar. Cool. Add puree and juice. Place in freezer until mushy. Stir every ½ hour until it is almost solid. Place in chilled bowl, and beat until smooth. Refreeze until solid in covered pan.

RASPBERRY ICE

½ cup sugar
½ cup water
1 quart ripe raspberries
1 cup water

Prepare syrup by boiling sugar with water. Cool. Mash berries, straining out seeds in fine sieve. Pour water through sieve to obtain more pulp. Add syrup. Freeze as above.

Serve in honeydew halves with melon balls for garnish.

Fennel Cookies

Yield: 4 dozen. Oven 375°F. Cookie sheet, greased.

⅓ cup margarine
⅓ cup butter
1⅔ cups sugar
¼ tsp. baking soda
2 eggs, beaten
3½ cups flour
2 tsp. baking powder
3 Tbs. fennel (or caraway, poppy, sesame, or anise) seeds
egg white
cinnamon and sugar mixture

Mix shortenings, sugar, and soda. Add other ingredients. Drop by teaspoons on cookie sheet. Press down with bottom of a glass wrapped in a floured cloth.

Brush with egg white and sprinkle cinnamon sugar on top. Bake 12 minutes. These are better if allowed to ripen a day or two.

BIRTHDAY DINNER

Eggplant and Pine Nut Dip

Steak

Stuffed Summer Squash

Filled Angel Food Cake

Strawberries

Eggplant and Pine Nut Dip

Oven 400°F.

1 large eggplant
2 green onions, chopped
1 Tbs. lemon juice
2 cloves garlic, chopped
½ tsp. salt
⅛ tsp. pepper
½ cup plain yogurt
½ cup pine nuts
2 Tbs. chopped parsley
1 Tbs. chopped fresh mint

Bake eggplant in pie plate until soft. Skin, and blend in food processor with other ingredients.

Serve on romaine leaves or grape leaves as a first course, or with crackers or pita bread as a dip.

Stuffed Summer Squash

Serves 6. Oven 375°F.

3 summer squash
½ cup chopped onion
1 or 2 cloves garlic, pressed
2 Tbs. butter
½ cup chopped parsley
2 large tomatoes, chopped, or 16-oz. can tomatoes, drained
1 cup cooked rice
1 cup corn, fresh or frozen
Parmesan cheese, grated

Steam squash whole for 10 minutes. Cut in half. Scoop out centers and chop. Sauté onion and garlic in butter. Mix with squash centers, and add remaining ingredients. Cook for a few minutes. Salt and pepper to taste. Stuff shells and top with grated cheese. Bake for 20 minutes.

Filled Angel Food Cake

Serves 6-8.

1 angel food cake	With sharp knife, carefully hollow cake, leaving a shell about 1 inch thick. Cut the removed cake into small pieces.
4 eggs **1½ cups sugar** **¼ cup lemon juice** **½ cup orange juice** **1 tsp. lemon rind** **2 tsp. orange rind** **2 cups whipped cream** **1 tsp. vanilla**	Beat eggs with 1 cup sugar, the juices, and rinds. Cook and stir over hot water until thick. Cool. When cold, fold in 1 cup whipped cream and cake pieces. Spoon into cake shell, and chill until firm. Add remaining sugar and vanilla to rest of whipped cream, and frost cake just before serving.
whole strawberries	Serve with strawberries.

LABOR DAY COOKOUT

Vegetable Curry Dip

Broiled Chicken with Spicy Sauce

Beet and Rice Salad

Zucchini Bread

New England Apple Pie

Vegetable Curry Dip

2 cups mayonnaise
3 Tbs. minced onion
1 Tbs. honey
3 Tbs. tomato paste
1 Tbs. curry powder
Tabasco to taste

Combine and serve with raw vegetables.

Spicy Sauce for Broiled Chicken

½ cup butter
1½ cups hot water
2 Tbs. vinegar
¼ tsp. salt
dash pepper
¼ tsp. paprika
¼ tsp. chili powder
1 tsp. sugar
2 tsp. prepared mustard
¼ tsp. Worcestershire sauce
1 Tbs. chopped onion
few drops Tabasco

Simmer all ingredients in saucepan. Baste on chicken as it is broiled.

Beet and Rice Salad

Serves 6-8.

¾ cup raw rice
2 cups diced, cooked beets
¼ cup finely chopped onion
½ cup French dressing
1½ cups mayonnaise
(celery, green beans, or broccoli, chopped)

Cook rice. Combine with beets in a bowl. Stir in onion and French dressing. Chill at least 24 hours. Stir in mayonnaise before serving, and add other vegetables as desired.

Zucchini Bread

Oven 325°F. 2 loaf pans, greased.

3 eggs
1 cup vegetable oil
2 cups brown sugar
2 cups grated zucchini
3 cups flour (can combine white and whole wheat)
1 tsp. vanilla
1 tsp. baking soda
1 tsp. salt
1 tsp. baking powder
1 tsp. cinnamon
½ cup chopped nuts
½ cup chopped dates

Beat eggs well, and mix in other ingredients. Bake 1 hour.

New England Apple Pie

Oven 400°F. 9-inch pie pan.

CRUST
⅔ cup vegetable shortening
2 cups flour
½ tsp. salt
ice water, about 5 Tbs.

FILLING
6 or 7 tart apples, cored and peeled
1 cup sugar
1 Tbs. flour
1 tsp. cinnamon
¼ tsp. nutmeg
¼ tsp. salt
½ tsp. ground cloves
3 Tbs. butter

GARNISH
ice cream
Cheddar cheese

Cut shortening into flour and salt until size of small peas. Add ice water gradually until flour has been absorbed, and dough forms a ball. Handle as little as possible. Divide in half. Roll out on floured board to size just a little larger than pie plate. Fit into plate and trim edges to fit outside rim. Slice apples onto bottom crust, making a compact filling. Mound up slightly in center. Mix sugar, flour, and spices. Sprinkle sugar mixture evenly over apples. Dot with butter.

Roll out top crust, cover apples, and trim to ½-inch overhang to tuck under bottom crust. Press both crusts together around edge of plate with a 4-tined fork to seal in juice. Slash crust in a pretty design to allow steam to escape. Bake on top rack 15 minutes. Place on lower rack, and bake at 325°F. for an additional 30-35 minutes. For the All-American favorite dessert, serve warm with scoops of vanilla ice cream or chunks of good sharp nibbling cheese.

Autumn

BELKNAP HOUSE
ANNIVERSARY BUFFET

Champagne Strawberry Punch

Stuffed Mushrooms

Chicken Almond Spread

Seafood Newburg

Rice

Baked Ham

Green Vegetable Platter

Currant Buns

White Chocolate Mousse

The Anniversary Party celebrates September 15, 1978, the day Belknap House opened its doors to its first residents.

Champagne Strawberry Punch

Serves 10-12. Large punch bowl.

3 cups fresh whole strawberries
½ gallon sauterne or Rhine wine, chilled
1 bottle champagne, chilled

Marinate strawberries in 1 cup of the wine for a few hours. Make an ice ring, with some strawberries, if desired. Combine chilled wines, ice ring, and strawberries in a serving bowl.

Stuffed Mushrooms

Oven 400°F. Cookie sheet, greased.

12 big mushrooms
2 tsp. butter
1 Tbs. butter
¼ lb. bacon, chopped
1 small onion, minced
1 cup white bread crumbs
1 cup grated sharp Cheddar cheese
¼ cup milk, or just enough to bind ingredients

Chop mushroom stems finely, and sauté in 2 tsp. butter. Sauté caps in 1 Tbs. butter for 10 minutes. Reserve any liquid for stuffing. Fry bacon, remove, and drain. Sauté onion in 1 Tbs. bacon fat. Add crumbs, bacon, chopped mushroom stems, cheese, milk, and reserved mushroom liquid, if needed. Divide stuffing evenly into mushroom caps. Bake for 10-15 minutes, or until bubbly.

GARNISH:
pimiento bits and parsley

Garnish as suggested, and serve hot.

Chicken Almond Spread

1 cup ground cooked chicken
1 cup ground toasted almonds, or pecans
1 Tbs. minced parsley
mayonnaise to make smooth paste
salt and pepper

Mix spread ingredients.

biscuits, or bread rounds

Serve on tiny hot biscuits or rounds of bread, sautéed on one side.

Seafood Newburg

Serves 4-6.

3 Tbs. butter
3 Tbs. flour
1½ cups milk
¼ tsp. salt
dash pepper
1 egg yolk
⅓ cup dry white wine
3 cups mixed cooked seafood — lobster, shrimp, scallops, and fish
2 Tbs. chopped fresh parsley
½ tsp. tarragon
rice

Melt butter and stir in flour. Cook 1 minute, then stir in milk. Cook, still stirring, until thickened. Add salt and pepper. Beat egg yolk lightly. Add a little hot sauce to yolk, then return to rest of sauce and blend well.
Add wine, fish, and herbs. Heat through. Serve with rice.

Green Vegetable Platter

1 bunch fresh broccoli
½ lb. fresh green beans
½ lb. fresh snow peas

Steam vegetables briefly in separate batches. Combine dressing ingredients. Arrange vegetables on platter, and pour dressing over. Serve at room temperature.

DRESSING
½ cup oil
¼ cup wine vinegar
pinch sugar
salt and pepper

Currant Buns

Yield: 12 large buns. Oven 375°F.

1 cup milk
4 Tbs. butter
1 package yeast
2 cups flour
¼ tsp. salt
2 eggs
½ cup sugar
¼ cup currants
1 egg white and 1 Tbs. sugar

Scald milk with butter, and cool to lukewarm. Add yeast, flour, and salt. Let rise in refrigerator overnight. In morning, add eggs, sugar, and currants. Let rise for 3-4 hours. Shape flat rolls, and place in greased pan almost touching. Brush tops with egg white mixture. Let rise until double, and bake for 20 minutes.

White Chocolate Mousse

Serves 8. Individual dessert dishes, or 2-quart mold.

2 cups milk
½ cup sugar
8 oz. white chocolate
1 envelope plain gelatin
4 Tbs. cold milk
2 egg whites
½ cup confectioners' sugar
½ tsp. salt
1 cup whipping cream, beaten
¼ cup crème de cacao

crème de menthe

GARNISH
toasted sliced almonds

Scald milk in double boiler. Add sugar and chocolate, and stir until dissolved. Soften gelatin in cold milk. Dissolve in hot milk. Cool to soft jell. Beat egg whites until stiff with sugar and salt. Fold crème de cacao into whipped cream. Combine three mixtures very gently. Pour into dishes or mold. Chill. For a special touch put a teaspoon of crème de menthe on top.

Garnish as suggested.

BUSY DAY FAMILY SUPPER

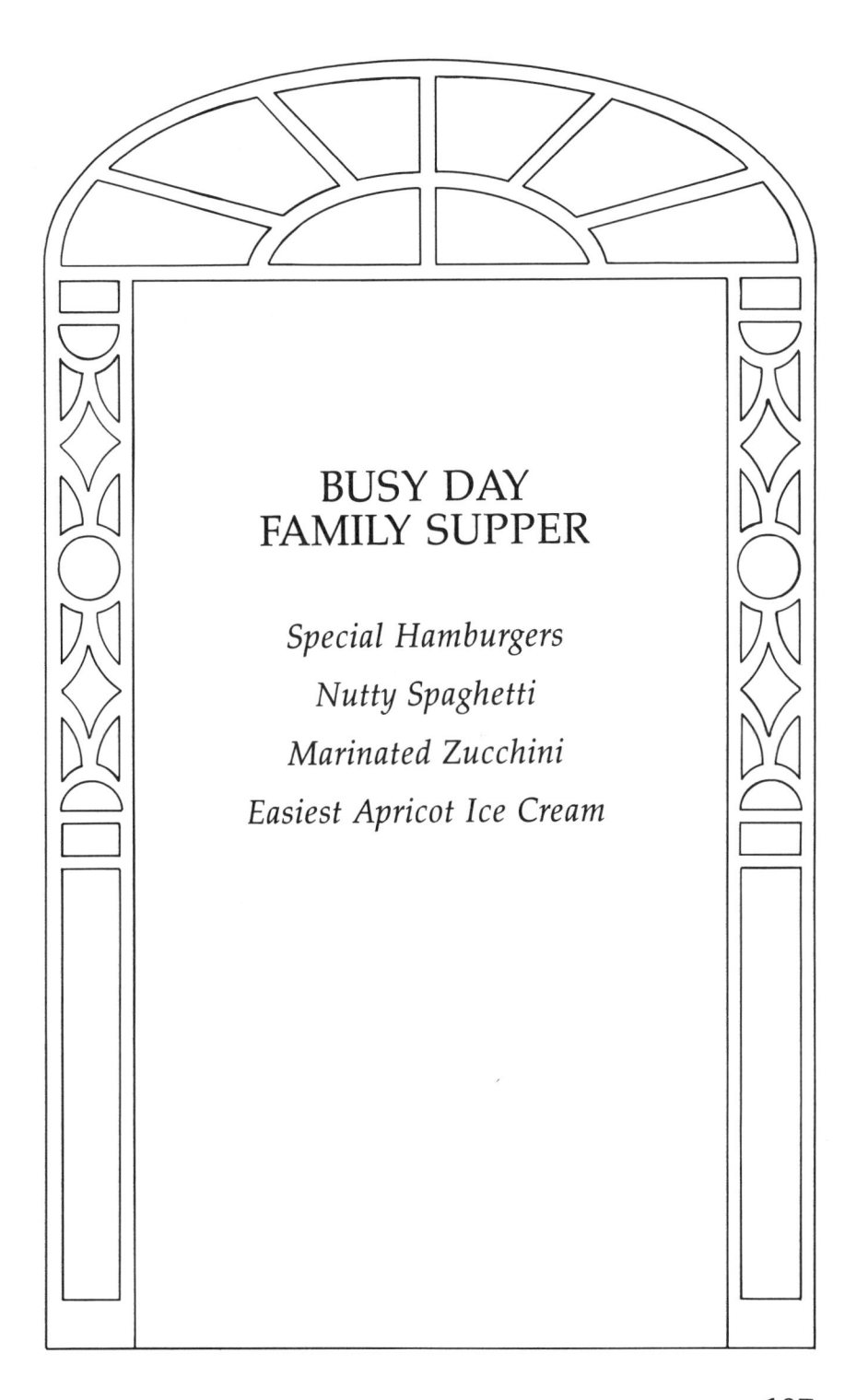

Special Hamburgers

Nutty Spaghetti

Marinated Zucchini

Easiest Apricot Ice Cream

Special Hamburgers

Serves 4.

1 lb. ground sirloin, shaped in patties
3 Tbs. butter
¾ cup wine, either red or white, each will have its flavor
fresh herbs — tarragon or chervil

Sauté ground beef patties in 1 Tbs. butter. Remove meat to hot platter. Add 2 more Tbs. butter to skillet, add wine and herbs, and cook until most of liquid has evaporated. Pour over meat, and serve.

Nutty Spaghetti

1 clove garlic, pressed
3 Tbs. oil
salt and pepper
⅔ cup chopped walnuts
½ cup chopped black olives
½ cup chopped green stuffed olives
½ cup chopped fresh parsley
1 Tbs. fresh basil
1 lb. spaghetti
grated Parmesan cheese

Sauté garlic in oil. Mix together next 6 ingredients. Cook spaghetti as directed on package. Drain. Add nut mixture, and toss all together. Serve with grated Parmesan cheese.

Marinated Zucchini

4 medium zucchini, sliced
1 clove garlic, chopped
4 Tbs. olive oil
salt and pepper
1 Tbs. fresh dill, or ½ tsp. dried
3 Tbs. wine vinegar

Sauté zucchini and garlic in oil until golden. Toss in bowl with other ingredients and let marinate 4 hours before serving. Serve on lettuce.

This will keep 2 weeks in covered jar in refrigerator.

Easiest Apricot Ice Cream

Yield: 1 quart.

2 cups buttermilk
1½ cups apricot jam (or peach or raspberry)

Stir buttermilk into jam. Pour into freezer tray. Freeze until firm. Cut up mixture and place in chilled mixer bowl. Beat until fluffy. Return to tray and freeze until firm.

GARNISH
chopped almonds

Garnish as suggested.

SUPPER AFTER WALKING IN THE ESTABROOK WOODS

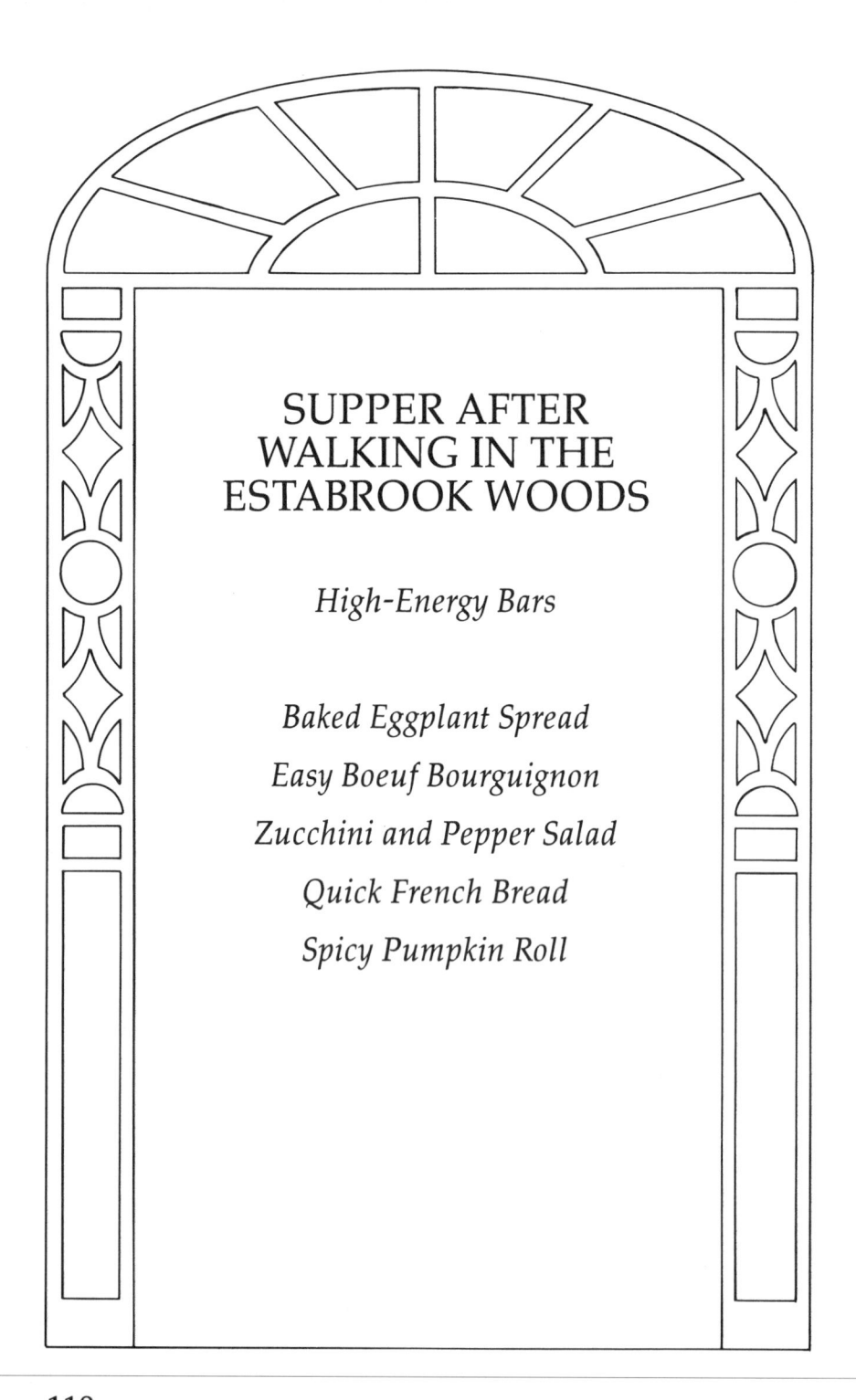

High-Energy Bars

Baked Eggplant Spread

Easy Boeuf Bourguignon

Zucchini and Pepper Salad

Quick French Bread

Spicy Pumpkin Roll

High-Energy Bars

Yield: 12 bars. Oven 350°F. 8-inch square pan, greased.

½ cup butter or margarine ¾ cup brown sugar ½ cup oats ½ cup whole wheat flour ½ cup all purpose flour ¼ cup wheat germ 2 tsp. grated orange rind 2 eggs, beaten 1 cup whole blanched almonds ¼ cup raisins ¼ cup coconut ½ cup semisweet chocolate bits	Cream butter and sugar. Add oats, flours, wheat germ, and rind. Pat into pan. Mix eggs, almonds, raisins, coconut, and chocolate bits. Pour over crust, and bake for 35 minutes. When cool, cut and wrap in plastic to keep moist. These should be made ahead to take on the hike.

Baked Eggplant Spread

Oven 350°F. 1-quart casserole, greased.

1 eggplant 2 onions, chopped ½ green pepper, chopped 2 Tbs. olive oil ½ can tomato paste 1 Tbs. lemon juice 1 Tbs. sugar salt and pepper to taste	Bake eggplant until very soft. Peel and chop. Brown onions and pepper in olive oil until soft. Mix with eggplant and other ingredients and blend. Turn into casserole, and bake for 1 hour, or to a good spreading consistency. Chill.

GARNISH
chopped hard-boiled egg
fresh dill

Serve cold, garnished as suggested, with crackers or pumpernickel slices.

Easy Boeuf Bourguignon

Serves 6. Oven 250°F.

2 lbs. beef, cubed
4 carrots, thickly sliced
1 cup chopped celery
2 onions, sliced
2 cups canned tomatoes
1 clove garlic, pressed
3 Tbs. minute tapioca
1 Tbs. sugar
½ cup Burgundy wine
1 bay leaf
½ tsp. each, thyme and sage
salt and pepper
1 cup sliced water chestnuts
1 cup sliced mushrooms
two 1-lb. cans small Irish potatoes

Combine all ingredients except last 3 in large casserole. Bake for 4 hours.

Add last 3 ingredients and cook 1 more hour. Can be refrigerated or frozen and reheated.

Zucchini and Pepper Salad

1 clove garlic, chopped
3 Tbs. oil
1 cup thin zucchini strips
1 red onion in rings
1 cup sweet red pepper strips
1 Tbs. fresh basil or tarragon
salt and pepper
1 Tbs. lemon juice
tomatoes, thickly sliced

Sauté garlic lightly in oil. Add zucchini, onion rings, and pepper strips. Cook 2 minutes. Add herbs, seasonings, and lemon juice. Chill.

Serve on tomato slices.

Quick French Bread

Oven 450°F. Trough pan, well greased. To freeze: bake for only 15 minutes. To reheat: brush with salted water and heat 10 minutes at 450°F.

1½ cups warm water 1 Tbs. honey 1½ tsp. salt 4½ Tbs. yeast **4 cups unbleached flour**	Mix water, honey, salt, and yeast. Let stand 10 minutes until bubbly. Add flour in small amounts until dough does not stick to bowl.

The dough should be extremely loose and sticky, unlike any other bread dough. *Resist* the urge to add more flour. Turn dough onto well-floured surface, and pat into oval with floured hands. Cut into 2-6 pieces depending on length of loaves. Roll each piece into a snake. Place in pan, cover with towel, and let rise 20 minutes in warm place.

Gash top of each loaf several times with sharp knife. Let rise again for 10 minutes. Brush with salted water. Place on middle shelf of hot oven. Bake 15-20 minutes or until bread begins to color. Remove from pans to cool.

Spicy Pumpkin Roll

Oven 350°F. 2 jelly-roll pans, greased, lined with wax paper, greased again.

6 eggs, separated
1 cup sugar
1-lb. can pumpkin
2 tsp. cinnamon
1 tsp. ginger
1 tsp. nutmeg
1 cup flour
1 tsp. baking powder

Beat egg whites until stiff, beating in ½ cup sugar. Beat egg yolks with ½ cup sugar. Add pumpkin, spices, flour, and baking powder. Fold in beaten egg whites. Spread in prepared pans. Bake 12 minutes. Cool.

FILLING

16 oz. softened cream cheese
1 cup sugar
1 Tbs. vanilla
1 cup finely chopped nuts

Combine filling ingredients and spread over dough. Roll up from long side. Freezes well.

HARVEST DINNER

Warm Smoked Beef and Cheese Dip

Pumpkin Soup

Cornish Game Hens

Corn on the Cob

Tomatoes Stuffed with Cucumbers

Bran-Buttermilk Muffins

Steamed Cranberry Pudding

Warm Smoked Beef and Cheese Dip

Oven 350°F. Small casserole.

8 oz. softened cream cheese
16 oz. cottage cheese
5 oz. smoked beef, chopped
dash onion powder
salt
Worcestershire sauce to taste
dash Tabasco
pecan halves

Mix all ingredients except pecans and place in casserole. Arrange pecans over top. Cover and bake 10 minutes.

Serve warm with crackers.

Pumpkin Soup

1 medium-sized pumpkin for each 3 cups pulp add:
1 cup milk
13-oz. can evaporated milk
4 Tbs. margarine
3 Tbs. brown sugar
1 tsp. salt
½ tsp. nutmeg
½ tsp. cinnamon
½ tsp. white pepper
½ tsp. ground cloves
⅛ tsp. saffron

GARNISH
chopped parsley or watercress

Wash pumpkin. Bake whole at 300°F. for 1 hour. Cool. Remove seeds, scrape pulp into bowl, and put through food mill. Combine with other ingredients in saucepan, and bring slowly just to boil. Turn down heat and allow to meld for 10 minutes. Add more milk if necessary, but mixture should be moderately thick.

Garnish as suggested.

Cornish Game Hens

Oven 400°F.

3 hens, split
½ cup Chablis
½ cup brandy
1 clove garlic, minced
1 small onion, minced
½ tsp. rosemary
½ tsp. tarragon

GARNISH

green grapes and parsley

Arrange hens in roasting pan, skin side up. Combine all other ingredients. Pour sauce over hens. Bake at 400°F. for ½ hour. Reduce heat to 325°F. for another 20 minutes. Baste occasionally. Roast until birds are tender when pierced with a fork.

Garnish as suggested.

Tomatoes Stuffed with Cucumbers

6 ripe tomatoes
2 cucumbers, chopped
1 small onion, sliced
½ cup vinegar
2 Tbs. sugar
2 Tbs. chopped parsley
1 small green pepper, chopped
½ cup water
1½ tsp. salt
¼ tsp. pepper

GARNISH

sour cream
fresh herbs — parsley, chives, dill

Skin, seed, and drain tomatoes. Mix all ingredients except tomatoes. Put in glass jar and chill. (May be kept up to 2 weeks.) Fill tomato shells.

Garnish as suggested.

Bran-Buttermilk Muffins

Yield: 1 gallon of batter. Oven 400°F. Muffin pans, greased.

2 cups boiling water
4 shredded-wheat biscuits
¾ cup shortening
3 cups sugar
4 eggs, beaten
4 cups bran or bran buds
1 quart buttermilk
5 tsp. baking soda
5 cups flour
1 tsp. salt
½ lb. raisins

Pour boiling water over shredded wheat. Set aside. In large bowl mix shortening and sugar. Add remaining ingredients, including softened shredded wheat. Mix well, but do not beat. Store in gallon jug in refrigerator overnight. May be kept up to 6 weeks. Fill muffin cups ⅔ full and bake 20 minutes, or until done.

Steamed Cranberry Pudding

Oven 350°F. 1-quart covered mold, greased.

2 tsp. baking soda
½ cup molasses
½ cup boiling water
1½ cups flour
1 tsp. baking powder
1 cup cranberries

SAUCE

½ cup sugar
½ cup cream
¼ cup butter

Mix soda, molasses, and boiling water. Add flour sifted with baking powder. Dredge cranberries with a little flour, and stir in. Cook in double boiler 15 minutes. Pour into mold and cover. Place mold in pan of water and steam in oven 2 hours. Blend sauce ingredients over low heat. Pour over pudding.

AUTUMN BRUNCH

Rosy Punch

Macedoine of Fruit

Rondeles with Roquefort

Broccoli Salad

Poppy Seed Muffins

Osgood Williams' Apple Cake

Rosy Punch

gingerale
cranberry juice
white wine

Mix in equal parts. Chill and serve over ice.

Macedoine of Fruit

½ cup dry vermouth
¼ cup sugar
¼ tsp. cinnamon
20 grapes, halved and seeded
4 navel oranges, sectioned
pineapple wedges
(other fruits of your choice)

Combine the first 3 ingredients and stir to dissolve sugar. Chill a few hours. Pour over fruit and marinate at least 1 hour.

Broccoli Salad

Serves 6.

1 bunch broccoli

DRESSING

¼ cup olive oil
¼ cup lemon juice
1 clove garlic, pressed
1 tsp. salt
⅛ tsp. pepper
1 Tbs. chopped parsley

Separate broccoli into flowers and steam until just tender. Drain and cool.

Combine dressing ingredients and marinate broccoli in dressing.
Serve on salad greens.

Poppy Seed Muffins

Yield: 20. Oven 400°F. Muffin tins, greased.

⅓ cup butter
½ cup sugar
1 egg
1½ cups flour
2½ tsp. baking powder
½ tsp. salt
¾ cup milk
¼ cup poppy seeds

Cream butter and sugar. Add egg and beat. Sift dry ingredients. Add alternately milk and poppy seeds. Mix just enough to moisten. Fill muffin cups ⅔ full. Bake for 20-25 minutes.

Rondeles with Roquefort

1 lb. veal, chicken, or turkey, ground
¼ lb. boiled ham, chopped
3 slices bread
⅓ cup heavy cream
½ cup butter
salt and pepper

WASH

1 egg
1 tsp. oil
1 tsp. water
bread crumbs

BUTTER TOPPING

¼ lb. unsalted butter
2-3 oz. Roquefort cheese
¼ cup finely chopped walnuts

This recipe is very simply made in a food processor. Grind meat. Soak bread in cream and squeeze dry. Cream butter. Combine with meat, bread, and seasoning. Shape into patties. (May be shaped into a log and frozen.)

Combine wash ingredients and brush over rondeles. Coat with crumbs, and sauté in additional butter.

Combine topping ingredients. Place a spoonful on top of each rondele. (Also very good on baked potatoes.)

Osgood Williams' Apple Cake

Oven 350°F. 8-inch square pan, greased.

2 Tbs. butter
½ cup sugar
½ tsp. cinnamon
½ tsp. nutmeg
1 tsp. vanilla
3 cups diced apple
¼ tsp. salt
1 tsp. baking soda
½ cup flour
1 egg

Mix all ingredients until well blended, and bake for 35-40 minutes.

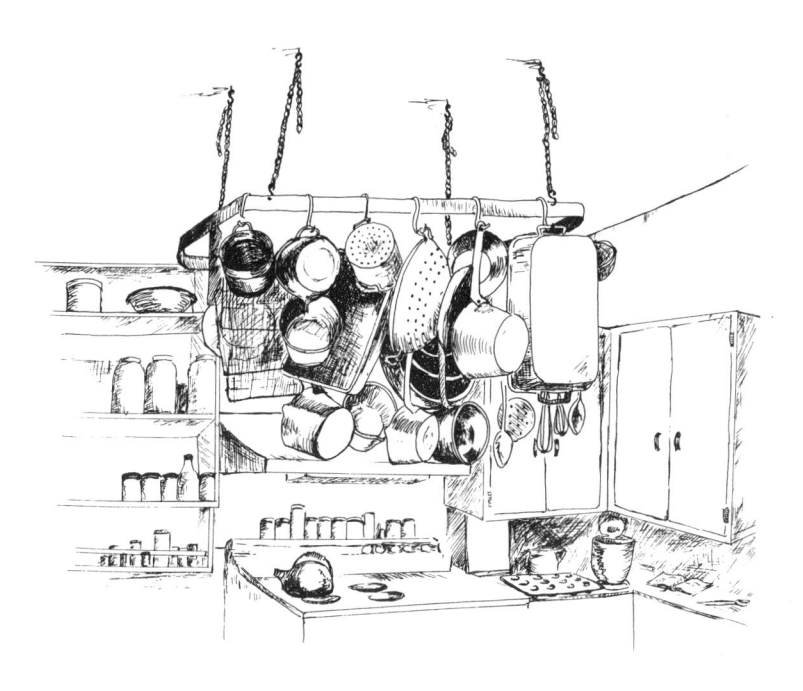

OPTIONAL TOPPING

whipped cream flavored with vanilla

BRIDGE LUNCHEON

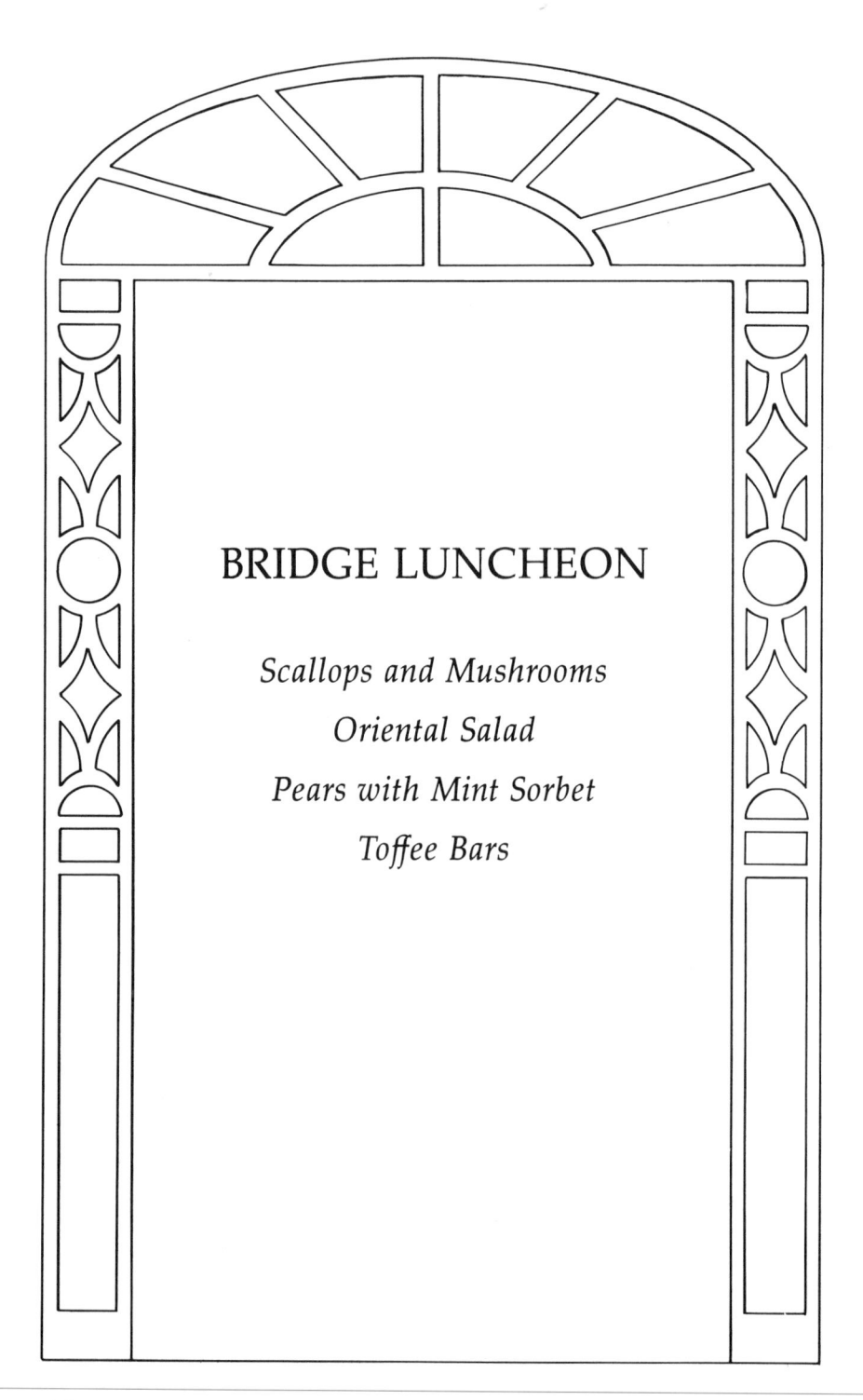

Scallops and Mushrooms

Oriental Salad

Pears with Mint Sorbet

Toffee Bars

Scallops and Mushrooms

Serves 4. Oven 400°F.

1 lb. mushrooms, sliced
5 Tbs. butter, divided
1 lb. sea scallops
¾ cup dry vermouth
¼ cup water
1 bay leaf
½ tsp. salt
⅛ tsp. pepper
3 Tbs. flour
1 cup light cream

Sauté sliced mushrooms in 2 Tbs. butter. Reserve. Wipe scallops with damp cloth. Put in skillet with wine, water, bay leaf, salt, and pepper. Simmer about 5 minutes until scallops are opaque. Do not overcook, as they will toughen. Remove bay leaf. Reserve 1 cup broth. Cut each scallop into 4 pieces. Make cream sauce with remaining 3 Tbs. butter, flour, broth, and cream. Stir until thickened. Add scallops and mushrooms. Place in ovenproof dish.

BUTTERED SOFT CRUMBS

3 slices white bread
1 or 2 Tbs. melted butter

Put bread in blender, and mix with butter. Sprinkle on top. Bake for 10 minutes until bubbly.

Oriental Salad

DRESSING

1 cup vegetable oil
¼ cup vinegar
⅓ cup catsup
1 tsp. salt
1 tsp. Worcestershire sauce
¼ cup sugar
medium onion, chopped

Mix all dressing ingredients in blender.

Toss with salad.

SALAD

10-oz. bag fresh spinach
8-oz. can water chestnuts, drained and chopped
2 cups bean sprouts

Pears with Mint Sorbet

1 cup boiling water
½ cup mint leaves, crushed
5 Tbs. lime juice
¼ cup granulated sugar
1 egg white, stiffly beaten
1 Tbs. crème de menthe

6 cooked or canned pear halves

Pour boiling water over mint leaves and infuse, covered, 10-15 minutes. Strain; stir in lime juice and sugar. Pour into refrigerator tray, and freeze until partially set around edges. Place frozen mixture in bowl and beat 1 minute, then fold in egg white and crème de menthe. Return to freezer, and stir occasionally until almost frozen. Spoon into pear halves to serve.

Toffee Bars

Prepare 3-5 days before serving. Oven 275°F. Jelly-roll pan, greased.

1 cup butter
1 cup sugar
2 cups flour
1 egg yolk
1 tsp. vanilla
1 egg white, beaten stiff
½ cup finely chopped walnuts

Cream together butter and sugar. Add flour, egg yolk, and vanilla; beat until blended. Spread in pan. Top with egg white and sprinkle with nuts. Bake for 70 minutes.

MEETING DAY

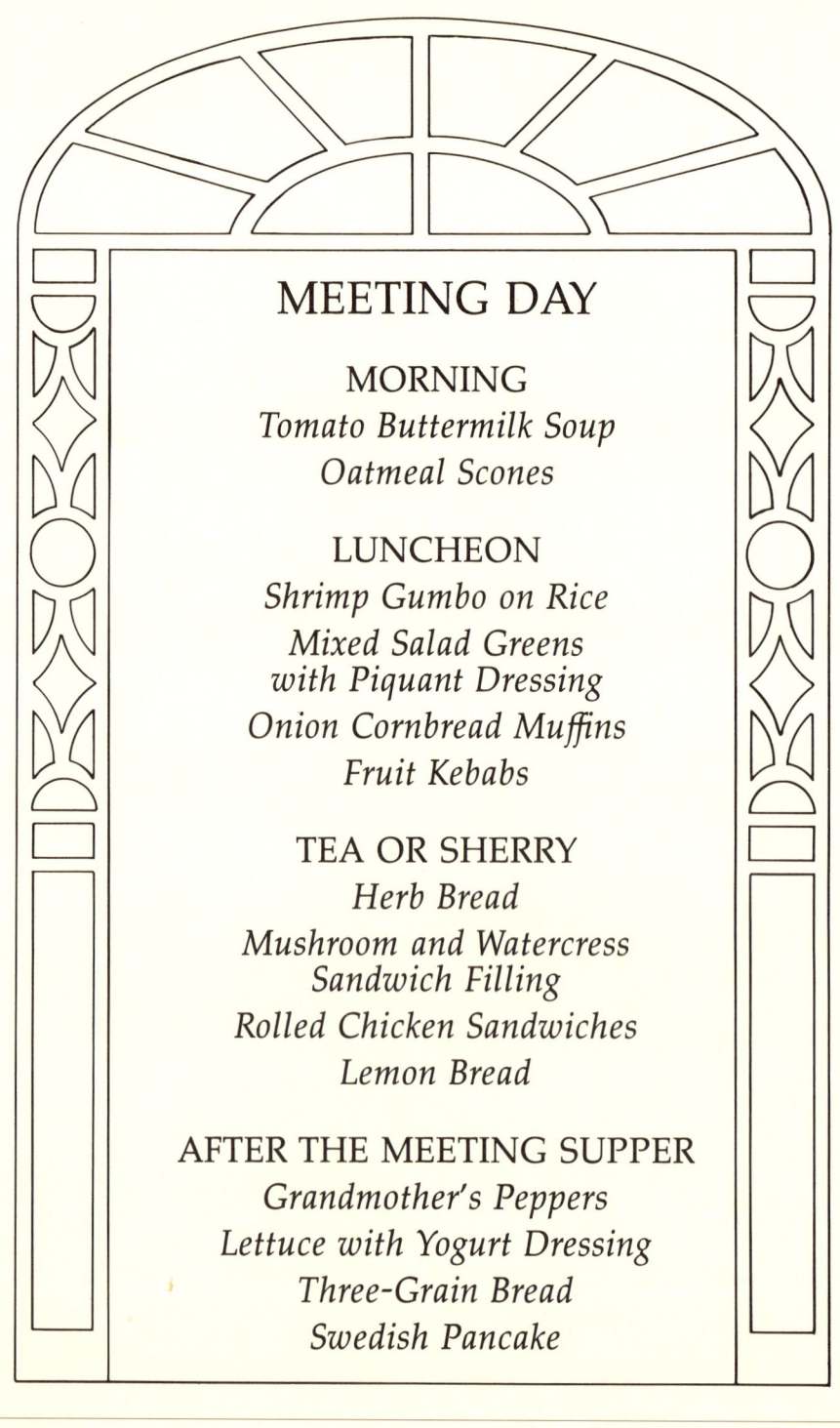

MORNING
Tomato Buttermilk Soup
Oatmeal Scones

LUNCHEON
Shrimp Gumbo on Rice
Mixed Salad Greens with Piquant Dressing
Onion Cornbread Muffins
Fruit Kebabs

TEA OR SHERRY
Herb Bread
Mushroom and Watercress Sandwich Filling
Rolled Chicken Sandwiches
Lemon Bread

AFTER THE MEETING SUPPER
Grandmother's Peppers
Lettuce with Yogurt Dressing
Three-Grain Bread
Swedish Pancake

Tomato Buttermilk Soup

Serves 6.

2 cups tomato juice
2 cups buttermilk
2 tsp. lemon juice
1 tsp. dill weed
¼ tsp. salt
⅛ tsp. garlic powder
⅛ tsp. onion powder

Combine all ingredients and heat. Do not boil. Can also be served chilled.

Oatmeal Scones

Yield: 16 scones. Oven 425°F. Cookie sheet, greased.

3 cups flour
3 cups rolled oats
¼ cup finely chopped walnuts
1½ tsp. salt
1½ tsp. baking soda
3 tsp. cream of tartar
3 Tbs. sugar
¾ cup butter
1½ cups milk

Mix dry ingredients. Cut in butter. Add milk and mix to form a soft dough. Divide dough into 3 parts. Pat each third on a floured board to form a round ½ inch thick. Cut each into 5 or 6 wedges. Bake for 15 minutes or until brown. Serve piping hot.

Shrimp Gumbo on Rice

Serves 6.

¼ cup margarine or oil
1 clove garlic, minced
2 onions, sliced
½ green pepper in strips
3 Tbs. flour
1 cup chicken stock
two 16-oz. cans tomatoes
1 tsp. salt
1 Tbs. Worcestershire sauce
¼ tsp. red pepper
2 lbs. raw shrimp
2 Tbs. gumbo filé powder
cooked rice with chopped parsley

Heat margarine or oil in large casserole, and sauté garlic, onions, and pepper. Stir in flour. Add stock, and whisk until smooth. Add tomatoes and seasonings.

Cook 20 minutes. Add shrimp and cook 3 minutes. Add filé powder to thicken.

Serve over rice.

Mixed Salad Greens

PIQUANT DRESSING

1 tsp. dry mustard
3 Tbs. walnut oil
1 Tbs. wine vinegar
2 Tbs. tarragon vinegar
3 Tbs. olive oil
1 tsp. tarragon

Mix piquant dressing. Toss with salad.

SALAD

endive, escarole, chicory, grated carrots, cauliflowerets

Onion Cornbread Muffins

Yield: 18 muffins. Oven 375°F. Muffin tins, well greased.

1 cup stone-ground graham flour
1 cup yellow corn meal
4 tsp. baking powder
½ tsp. salt
2 Tbs. finely chopped onion
2 eggs
1⅓ cups milk
¼ cup honey
¼ cup cooking oil

Measure flour into large bowl. Add other dry ingredients and onion. Beat eggs and mix with milk, honey, and oil. Add liquids to dry ingredients, and stir until well blended. Fill muffin pan cups ⅓ full. Bake for 12-15 minutes.

Fruit Kebabs

diced pineapple
orange sections
diced apples
grapes

Place bite-sized pieces of fruit on wooden skewers.

Herb Bread

Yield: 1 loaf. Oven 375°F. 9-inch loaf pan, greased.

1 package yeast
¼ cup warm water
2 tsp. sugar
8 oz. large-curd cottage cheese
2 Tbs. melted butter
1 egg
2 tsp. minced onion
2 tsp. salt
¼ tsp. baking soda
2 tsp. dill
1 cup cracked or whole wheat flour
1½ cups all purpose flour

Dissolve yeast in water and sugar and let stand for 5 minutes. Beat with all ingredients except flours. Add flours and knead for 5 minutes. Shape loaf and let rise in pan until double. Bake for 35 minutes, or until loaf sounds hollow when tapped with knuckles.

Mushroom and Watercress Sandwich Filling

1 large onion, chopped
3 Tbs. butter
¾ lb. mushrooms, chopped
3 large bunches watercress, chopped
8 oz. cream cheese, softened
pinch salt
dash Tabasco

Sauté onion in butter until transparent. Remove and sauté mushrooms. Add watercress and stir until limp. Mix with remaining ingredients in blender or food processor until smooth. Chill and use as a spread.

Rolled Chicken Sandwiches

Yield: 3 dozen.

36-40 thin slices white bread
three 3-oz. packages cream cheese
2 cups packed ground, cooked chicken or turkey
½ cup finely chopped celery
¼ cup chopped parsley
½ cup dry white wine
1 tsp. grated onion
1 tsp. Worcestershire sauce
salt and pepper
softened butter

Remove crusts from bread. Have cheese at room temperature. Combine chicken, celery, and parsley with cheese. Add other ingredients except butter. Roll bread with rolling pin, spread with softened butter, then chicken mixture. Roll. Cover and chill at least 3 hours. Can be made day before or frozen.

Lemon Bread

Yield: 1 loaf. Oven 350°F.

½ tsp. salt
6 Tbs. shortening
1 cup sugar
2 eggs
grated rind of 1 lemon
1½ cups flour
2 tsp. baking powder
½ cup chopped nuts

Mix in given order. Do not overbeat. Bake for 1 hour.

SYRUP

juice of 1 lemon
⅓ cup sugar

Boil lemon juice with sugar. Pour over warm bread. Cool in pan.

Grandmother's Peppers

Serves 4. Oven 350°F.

4 green peppers, halved and seeded
(½ lb. hamburger)
1-lb. can kidney beans
1 large onion, chopped
1 cup rice, parboiled
6-oz. can tomato paste
beef stock

Place peppers in greased casserole. Brown optional hamburger. Mix with other ingredients and put over peppers. Add stock to cover. Bake 1 hour.

Three-Grain Bread

Yield: 1 loaf. Oven 350°F. 9-inch loaf pan, greased.

1½ cups stone-ground graham flour
2 cups white flour
2 tsp. baking soda
½ tsp. salt
½ cup dark brown sugar
¾ cup bran buds
½ cup molasses
2 cups buttermilk

Put graham flour in bowl. Sift white flour, soda, and salt into it. Add sugar and bran. Stir in liquid ingredients. Turn batter into loaf pan. Bake for 1 hour and 10 minutes.

Yogurt Dressing

8 oz. yogurt
1½ Tbs. claret wine
3 Tbs. salad oil
1 clove garlic, pressed
1 tsp. salt
1 tsp. paprika
dash Tabasco

Shake all ingredients together in a jar. Serve on lettuce.

Swedish Pancake

Serves 4. Oven 375°F. 9-inch skillet.

2 Tbs. butter
⅔ cup flour
½ tsp. salt
2 eggs, beaten
1 cup milk

Melt butter in skillet in oven. Mix remaining ingredients until smooth. Pour into pan. Bake 30 minutes. This will puff up like a popover, but fall rapidly.

GARNISH

powdered sugar and jam
sliced fruit and whipped cream
lemon wedges

Garnish as suggested and serve immediately.

CHARADES PARTY

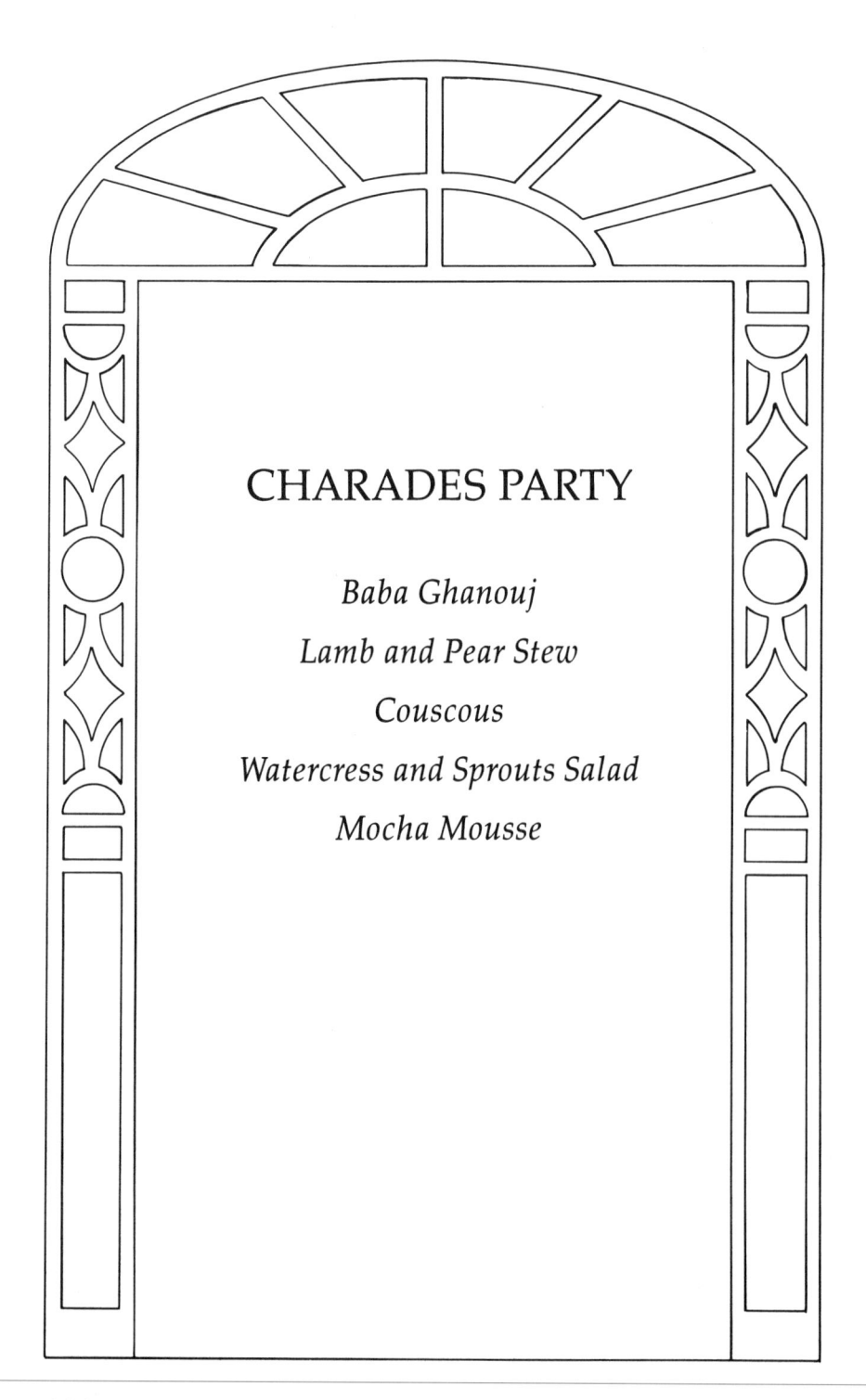

Baba Ghanouj

Lamb and Pear Stew

Couscous

Watercress and Sprouts Salad

Mocha Mousse

Baba Ghanouj

Oven 400°F.

1 large eggplant
¼ cup lemon juice
¼ cup sesame tahini
1 large clove garlic

Put eggplant in greased pan, prick skin, and bake for 45 minutes. Pull off skin when cool. Put pulp in blender with other ingredients. Process until well blended. Let stand a few hours before serving to develop flavor. Serve with pita bread or raw vegetables.

Lamb and Pear Stew

Serves 6.

⅓ cup flour
½ tsp. sugar
1½ tsp. salt
½ tsp. ground ginger
2½ lbs. boneless lamb, cubed
2 Tbs. melted butter
1 medium onion, chopped
1 cup dry white wine
1½ cups boiling water
6 whole seckel pears, peeled, or 12 dried-pear halves
1 lb. green beans
salt and pepper

Combine flour, sugar, salt, and ginger in bag. Shake lamb cubes in bag. Brown slowly in dutch oven in butter with onion. Add wine and water. Cover and simmer. After 45 minutes, add pears and simmer 30 minutes longer. (Simmer Bartlett pears only 20 minutes.) Add beans to simmer the last 10 minutes. Season with salt and pepper, and serve with couscous or rice.

Watercress and Sprouts Salad

watercress
alfalfa sprouts

Toss together.

YOGURT DRESSING

1 cup yogurt, or buttermilk
1 cup cottage cheese
1½ tsp. vinegar
½ tsp. salt
¼ tsp. garlic powder
1 tsp. dill, or other herbs

Beat dressing ingredients together. Pour over greens just before serving.

Mocha Mousse

Serves 10-12. 1-quart soufflé dish with 4-inch strip of wax paper taped around outside. Brush dish with oil.

1 envelope unflavored gelatin
¼ cup cold water
4 oz. semisweet chocolate
1 Tbs. instant coffee in ¼ cup water
6 egg yolks
¼ cup sugar
6 egg whites, stiffly beaten
2 cups whipping cream, stiffly beaten

GARNISH
chocolate curls
whipped cream

Soften gelatin in cold water. Melt chocolate in coffee over low heat. Off heat, add gelatin and stir until dissolved. Combine egg yolks and sugar in double boiler. Beat over hot water until thick and light. Blend in chocolate mixture and pour into bowl. When cool, fold in egg whites and whipped cream. Pour into soufflé dish and chill at least 3 hours.
Garnish as suggested.

KNITTING AND CROCHETING TEA

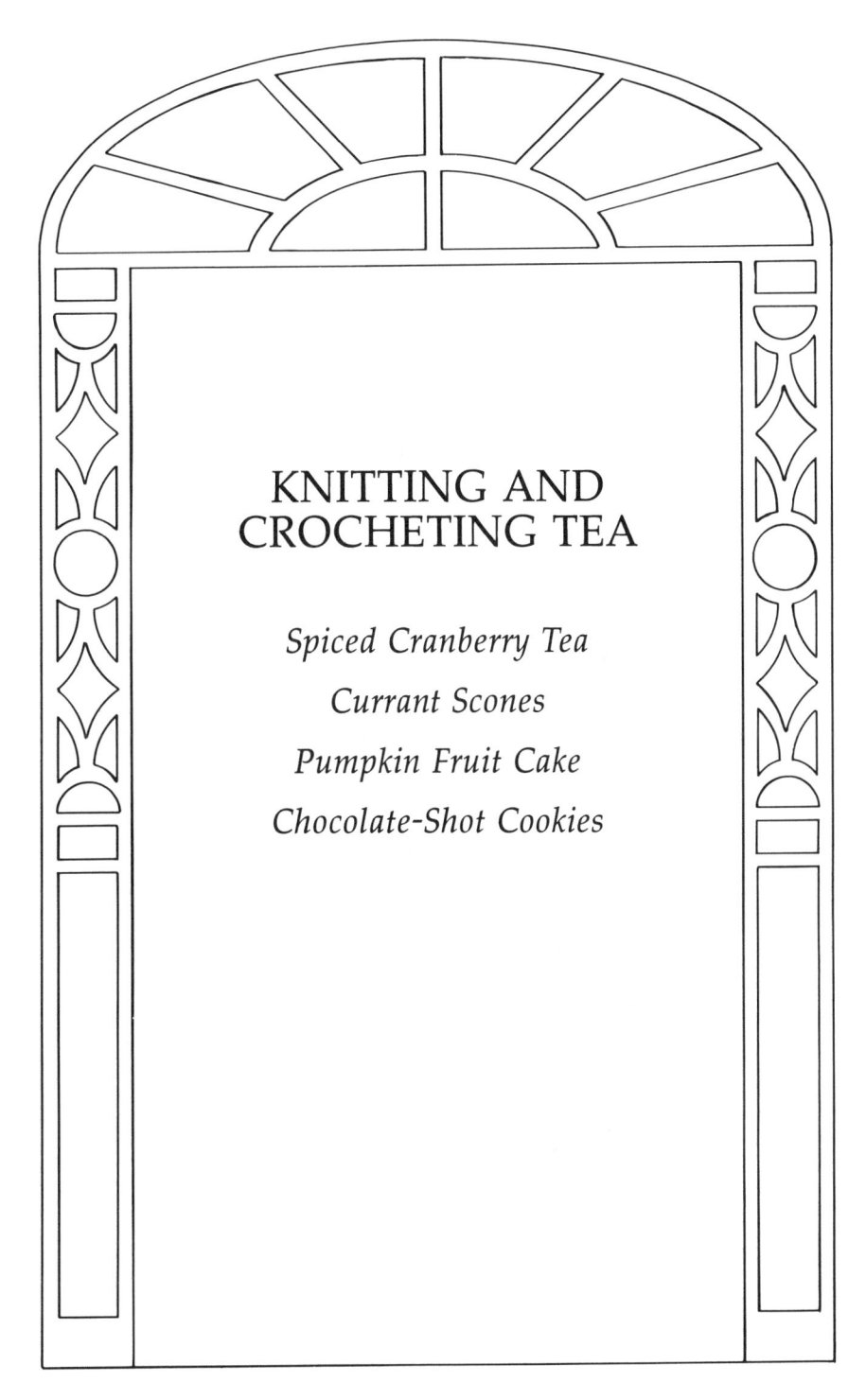

Spiced Cranberry Tea

Currant Scones

Pumpkin Fruit Cake

Chocolate-Shot Cookies

Spiced Cranberry Tea

Yield: 6 cups.

3 cups cranberry juice 3 cups water 2-oz. package lemon flavored iced-tea mix or 4 teabags and 2 Tbs. sugar lemon slices stuck with cloves cinnamon sticks	Simmer juice, water, and tea. Put a lemon slice and cinnamon stick in each serving mug, and pour in tea mixture. You may wish to simmer 2 cinnamon sticks and a few whole cloves with the tea mixture.

Currant Scones

Oven 425°F. Cookie sheet, greased.

3 cups flour 3 tsp. baking powder ¼ tsp. salt 1 tsp. sugar 1 or 2 Tbs. butter milk, enough to moisten ½ cup currants, or sultanas	Sift dry ingredients. Rub in butter. Add enough milk to make a soft dough. Add currants, and knead on a lightly floured board. Roll out ½ inch thick, cut into rounds, and bake for 10 minutes.

Pumpkin Fruit Cake

Oven 350°F. 10-inch tube pan, greased.

3 cups flour
½ tsp. salt
2½ tsp. baking powder
1½ tsp. baking soda
2 tsp. cinnamon
4 eggs
2 cups sugar
1¼ cups oil
2 cups cooked pumpkin
¾ cup raisins
¾ cup chopped walnuts

Sift dry ingredients together.

Beat eggs, add sugar, oil, and pumpkin, then dry ingredients. Add raisins and nuts. Put into pan and bake 1 hour or until done. Let cool in pan 20-30 minutes. Turn out on rack.

Chocolate-Shot Cookies

Oven 350°F.

1 cup shortening (part butter)
1 cup confectioners' sugar
2 tsp. vanilla
1½ cups flour
½ tsp. baking soda
½ tsp. salt
1½ cups rolled oats
chocolate shots ("jimmies")

Mix first 7 ingredients, and form into two rolls about 1¼ inches in diameter. Roll in chocolate shots to coat. Chill. Slice ¼ inch thick. Bake about 10 minutes.

BIRTHDAY DINNER

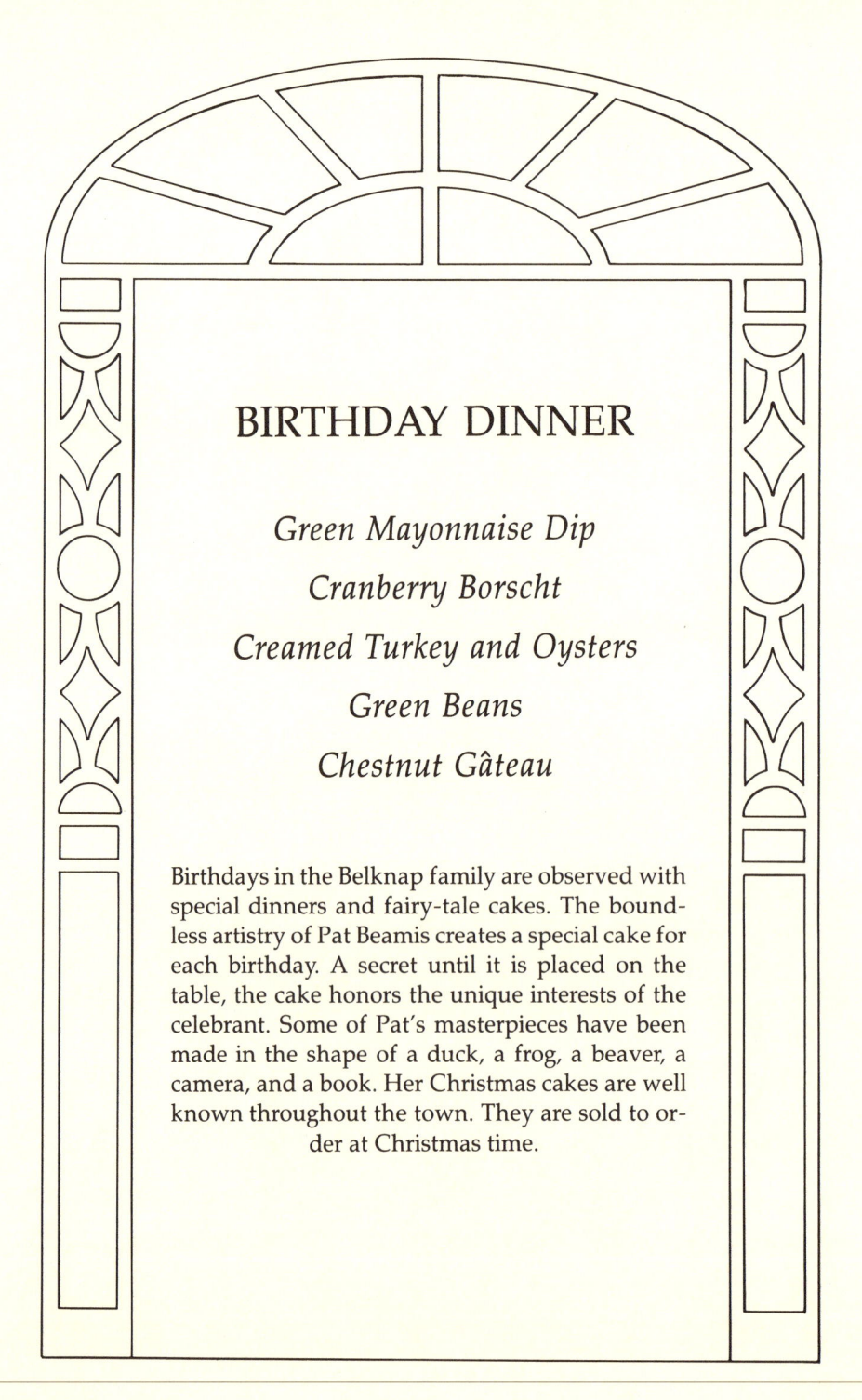

Green Mayonnaise Dip

Cranberry Borscht

Creamed Turkey and Oysters

Green Beans

Chestnut Gâteau

Birthdays in the Belknap family are observed with special dinners and fairy-tale cakes. The boundless artistry of Pat Beamis creates a special cake for each birthday. A secret until it is placed on the table, the cake honors the unique interests of the celebrant. Some of Pat's masterpieces have been made in the shape of a duck, a frog, a beaver, a camera, and a book. Her Christmas cakes are well known throughout the town. They are sold to order at Christmas time.

Green Mayonnaise Dip

½ tsp. sugar
½ cup parsley
1 cup spinach (10 leaves)
½ cup chives
1 cup watercress
1 egg
1 tsp. dry mustard
2 Tbs. wine vinegar
¼ cup oil
½ tsp. salt
dash pepper
¾ cup oil

Put all ingredients in blender except ¾ cup oil.

Add additional oil slowly, continuing to blend. Refrigerate. Serve with crackers or chips.

Cranberry Borscht

Serves 6-8.

½ cup chopped scallions, or shallots
1 Tbs. butter or margarine
2 cups cranberries
3 cups chicken broth
1-lb. can beets and juice, pureed
¼ cup sherry
½ tsp. pepper
¼ cup sugar

GARNISH
lemon slices
sour cream

Sauté scallions in butter.

Simmer cranberries in chicken broth 5 minutes. Puree in blender. Combine all ingredients and serve hot or cold, garnished with lemon slices or sour cream.

Creamed Turkey and Oysters in Toast Cups

Serves 8. Oven 325°F. Muffin pans, greased.

1 pint fresh oysters
6 Tbs. margarine
8 Tbs. flour
1 tsp. salt
½ tsp. white pepper
3 cups milk and oyster liquid combined
3 cups diced cooked turkey

Drain oysters. If large cut them in half. Set aside. Melt margarine; add flour and seasonings. Heat until mixture bubbles. Gradually add liquids and cook until sauce thickens, stirring. Add turkey and oysters.

TOAST CUPS

8 slices of very thin white bread, crusts removed

To limber bread: place between clean damp cloths on a cookie tray. Cover top with another tray and place in 325°F. oven for 15-20 minutes. Remove bread and butter it. Press gently into muffin pans to form shells. Bake at 350°F. for 12-15 minutes. Fill toast cups with creamed mixture.

Chestnut Gâteau

8-inch spring-form pan.

CAKE

- ¼ lb. plus 2 Tbs. butter
- 1½ cups confectioners' sugar
- 5 oz. sieved chestnuts (½ can pureed)
- 1 Tbs. cocoa
- 1 egg yolk
- 54 ladyfingers
- 1 cup strong coffee

Cream butter and sugar. Add chestnut puree, cocoa, and egg yolk. Put circle of wax paper on bottom of pan for easy removal. Dip ladyfingers in coffee and line bottom of pan. Cut fingers in pieces to fill all spaces. Spread ½ the butter cream over fingers. Arrange a second layer of coffee-dipped fingers on top and second layer of butter cream. Refrigerate for several hours.

FROSTING

- ⅔ cup heavy cream, whipped
- 2 egg whites, beaten until stiff
- 1 Tbs. superfine sugar
- 1 or 2 tsp. liqueur

Mix frosting ingredients. Cover cake and decorate with remaining ladyfingers.

PROGRESSIVE DINNER

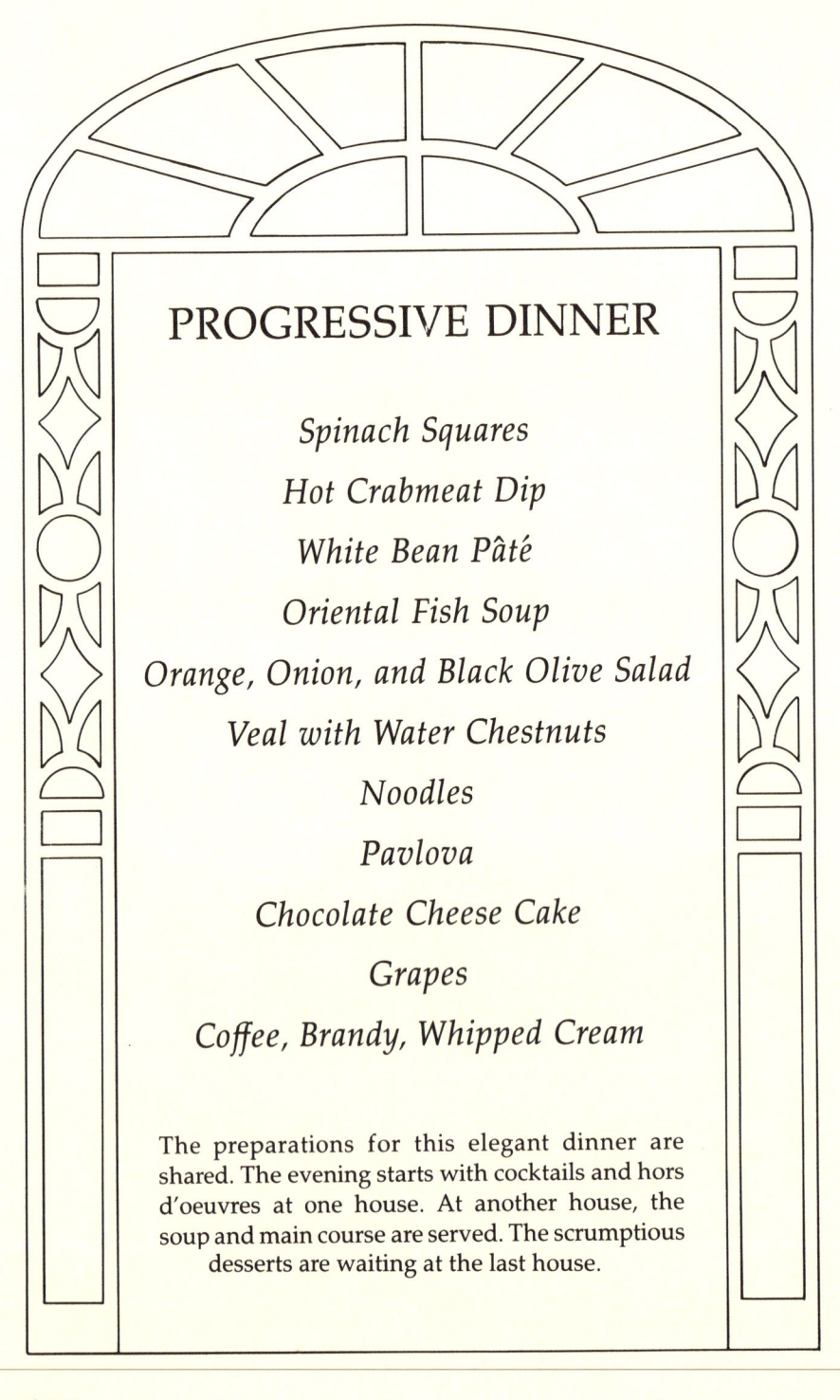

Spinach Squares

Hot Crabmeat Dip

White Bean Pâté

Oriental Fish Soup

Orange, Onion, and Black Olive Salad

Veal with Water Chestnuts

Noodles

Pavlova

Chocolate Cheese Cake

Grapes

Coffee, Brandy, Whipped Cream

The preparations for this elegant dinner are shared. The evening starts with cocktails and hors d'oeuvres at one house. At another house, the soup and main course are served. The scrumptious desserts are waiting at the last house.

Spinach Squares

Oven 350°F. 9x13-inch pan, greased.

4 Tbs. butter or margarine
3 eggs
1 cup flour
1 cup milk
1 tsp. salt
1 tsp. baking powder
1 lb. sharp Cheddar cheese, grated
1 Tbs. chopped onion
two 10-oz. packages frozen chopped spinach, thawed and drained
(seasoned salt)

Melt butter in pan. Beat eggs. Add flour, milk, salt, and baking powder. Mix in cheese, onion, and spinach. Spoon into pan and level off. Sprinkle with optional seasoned salt. Bake for 35 minutes. Let stand 45 minutes. Cut into small squares.

Freezes well. Defrost, then reheat at 325°F. for 12 minutes.

Hot Crabmeat Dip

Oven 375°F.

8-oz. package cream cheese, softened
1 Tbs. milk
8-oz. can crabmeat
1 Tbs. minced onion, or dry onion flakes
1 small clove garlic, crushed
2 tsp. horseradish
½ cup sliced almonds
salt and pepper

Combine ingredients in casserole. Bake for 15 minutes, or until bubbly. Serve with crackers.

White Bean Pâté

Oven 400°F. 1½-quart mold, greased.

3 Tbs. butter
2 cups grated carrots
3 cups cooked or canned Great Northern beans
2 egg yolks
⅔ cup bread crumbs
½ cup heavy cream
3 Tbs. each: melted butter, minced parsley, chopped scallions
1½ tsp. salt
pepper
¼ tsp. each: coriander, basil, thyme
2 egg whites, stiffly beaten
4 Tbs. melted butter

Sauté carrots in butter for 5 minutes. Cool and set aside. Puree beans. Beat yolks lightly; add to beans. Soak bread crumbs in cream. Add with seasonings to mixture. Fold in egg whites. Spoon ½ bean mixture into mold. Cover with 1 cup carrots and repeat. Pour melted butter over top. Cover with buttered wax paper, tied securely. Place mold on rack in pan with hot water ¾ to top of mold. Bake for 45 minutes. Cool 20 minutes and unmold. Serve warm.

Oriental Fish Soup

Serves 8. Heat-proof soup bowls.

3 cups chicken stock
2 scallions, chopped
2 tsp. finely chopped ginger root
1 cup dry sherry
1 lb. fillet of sole

GARNISH
parsley, chopped
lemon slices

Simmer first 4 ingredients together for 10 minutes. Cut fish into tiny pieces. Place bits in bowls. Just before serving, pour boiling broth over raw fish. Let stand 5 minutes. Serve, garnished as suggested.

Orange, Onion, and Black Olive Salad

FRENCH DRESSING

⅓ cup oil
2 Tbs. wine vinegar
½ tsp. mustard

Combine dressing ingredients in jar and shake well. Pour over salad and toss.

SALAD
orange sections
mild onion, sliced thinly
black olives
watercress

Veal with Water Chestnuts

Serves 8. Oven 375°F.

2 Tbs. butter
2½ lbs. veal, cubed
2 Tbs. butter
1 onion, chopped
1 clove garlic, minced
1 lb. mushrooms, sliced
1 tsp. salt
¼ tsp. pepper
1 cup beef broth
two 8-oz. cans water chestnuts, drained and sliced
2 bay leaves

1¾ cups heavy cream
¼ cup brandy
¼ cup chopped parsley
green noodles

Sauté veal in butter lightly. Remove. Add 2 more Tbs. butter and sauté onion, garlic, and mushrooms in same pan. Add salt, pepper, broth, water chestnuts, bay leaves, and veal. Cover and bake for 1½ hours. Remove bay leaves. Best made ahead to this point.

To serve, reheat at 350°F. with cream, brandy, and parsley. Serve over green noodles.

Pavlova

Serves 8. Oven 300°F. Cookie sheet.

MERINGUE

5 egg whites
¼ tsp. salt
1 tsp. vanilla
1 cup less 2 Tbs. sugar
1 tsp. vinegar
⅓ tsp. cream of tartar
3 Tbs. cornstarch

Beat egg whites until stiff with salt and vanilla. Beat in sugar gradually. Beat in vinegar, cream of tartar, and cornstarch. Line cookie sheet with heavy brown paper. Draw a 9-inch circle and spread mixture on it, building up the sides. Bake for 1 hour. Turn oven off and leave in oven 1 more hour or until dry. This is best made the day before.

FILLING

1 cup heavy cream, whipped
confectioners' sugar to taste

One or two hours before serving fill meringue with sweetened whipped cream. Chill.

GARNISH

kiwi fruit, or any fresh fruit in season

Decorate with fruit.

Chocolate Cheese Cake

Oven 325°F. Spring-form pan, greased.

CRUST

1 Tbs. sugar
¼ cup butter, melted
½ cup zwieback crumbs, or chocolate-cookie crumbs

Blend sugar, butter, and crumbs. Press crumbs into pan.

FILLING

8 oz. semisweet chocolate
1 Tbs. instant coffee
½ cup boiling water
two 8-oz. packages cream cheese, softened
¾ cup sugar
4 eggs
2 tsp. vanilla
1 cup heavy cream, whipped

Melt chocolate with coffee in water. Beat other ingredients well and add chocolate. Bake 1 hour. Cool at room temperature, then chill. Frost with whipped cream before serving.

GARNISH

chocolate curls

Garnish as suggested.

Winter

SUNDAY DINNER

Cheese Crispies

Tomato Aspic

Roast Beef

Yorkshire Pudding

Brussels Sprouts with Chestnuts

Plum Cake

The traditional Sunday dinner is served at noon in Belknap House.

Cheese Crispies

Yield: about 30. Oven 375°F. Cookie sheet, greased.

¼ lb. margarine
1 cup grated sharp cheese
1 cup flour
1 cup Rice Krispies
¼ cup sesame seeds, toasted
1 Tbs. Worcestershire sauce

Blend margarine and cheese, then add flour, Rice Krispies, sesame seeds, and seasoning. Roll into small balls, and place on cookie sheet. Flatten into thin rounds with fork. Bake for 10-12 minutes, or until slightly brown.

Tomato Aspic

1-quart mold.

2 Tbs. plain gelatin
4 cups V-8 juice
2 Tbs. red wine vinegar

Soften gelatin in ½ cup juice. Heat another ½ cup juice. Stir in gelatin off heat until dissolved. Add remaining juice and vinegar. Chill until set.

Yorkshire Pudding

Sunday Dinner at Gran's house was usually roast beef with Yorkshire pudding. The latter was my favorite food, so as a teenager I sought out the recipe. On my first try, I came out with a flat, pale, greasy pancake. So I went to Ida, Gran's cook at that time, and she gave me some educated advice. The next time I made it, it billowed so high and golden I thought it would escape from the oven. Her secret is in this recipe.

Gran also served "Goldenrod Eggs on Spinach," a dish of cooked spinach in a buttered cream sauce sprinkled with finely sieved hardboiled eggs.

Eleanor Motley Billings

Oven 400°F.

1 cup flour **1 cup milk at room temperature, or ⅓ cup powdered milk dissolved in 1 cup hot water** **2 eggs, room temperature**	Mix all ingredients with whisk. Take roast out of oven and raise temperature to 400°F.
pan of drippings from roast beef, or left-over steak drippings from broiler pan	Place pan of drippings back in oven until sizzling hot. Pour lukewarm batter into hot drippings. This is what makes it work. Bake for 25 minutes. Try not to peek while baking, for first 15 minutes.

Brussels Sprouts with Chestnuts

Serves 6.

½ lb. chestnuts, or 1 cup canned
1 lb. fresh or frozen Brussels sprouts
salt to taste
1 Tbs. butter

Slit skin on convex side of chestnuts. Boil for 3 minutes. Peel. Cover with water and boil for 20 minutes or until just tender. Cook sprouts in salted water until just tender and drain. Melt butter and sauté chestnuts for a few minutes. Add sprouts and toss to coat with butter.

Plum Cake

Serves 12. Oven 350°F. 10-inch tube pan, greased.

2 cups flour
2 tsp. baking powder
2 cups sugar
1 tsp. cinnamon
1 tsp. nutmeg
1 cup cooking oil
2 small jars strained plum and tapioca baby food
3 eggs
½ cup chopped nuts

SAUCE
¼ lb. butter
1 cup confectioners' sugar
juice and grated rind of one lemon

Stir ingredients together; do not beat. Bake for 1 hour. While cake is baking, make sauce.

Melt butter; stir in sugar, juice, and rind. Remove cake from oven. While still warm in pan, spread ½ sauce over cake and allow to soak in. Invert pan and remove cake while still warm. Spread remaining sauce on top.

WINTER BRUNCH

Bloody Mary

Chicken Livers with Apple Rings

Onion Pie

Molded Vegetable Salad

Orange Cake

Chicken Livers with Apple Rings

Serves 6-8.

2 large onions, chopped fine
2 Tbs. cooking oil or butter
1 cup sliced mushrooms
2 lbs. chicken livers
1 cup Chablis
½ cup sour cream
salt and pepper

Sauté onions in oil or butter. Add mushrooms and cook briefly. Remove from pan. Add more oil if necessary, and sauté livers until just brown; do not overcook. Return mushroom-onion mixture to pan. Add Chablis, cover pan, and simmer for 15 minutes. Season with salt and pepper to taste. Add sour cream just before serving, but do not allow to boil. Serve on rice, if desired.

APPLE RINGS

3 crisp apples, cored and sliced (Granny Smith is a good variety)
2 Tbs. butter
brown sugar
grenadine

Sauté unpeeled apples in butter. Sprinkle with brown sugar and grenadine.

Onion Pie

Serves 6-8. Oven 400°F. 9-inch pie pan.

CRUST

1½ cups fine Ritz cracker crumbs
⅓ cup margarine

Mix together crumbs and margarine and pat into pan.

FILLING

4 cups sliced onions
5 Tbs. margarine
2 eggs
1 cup creamy milk
salt and pepper
½ cup grated sharp cheese

Sauté onions in margarine until transparent. Beat eggs until light; add milk and seasonings. Pour into pie shell and put grated cheese on top. Bake about 20 minutes, or until custard is set and cheese is brown.

Molded Vegetable Salad

One-quart mold.

1 envelope plain gelatin
½ cup water
1¼ cups chicken stock
¼ cup vinegar
1 Tbs. lemon juice
¼ cup chopped scallions
1 cup chopped raw spinach
1 cup chopped celery
¼ cup shredded raw carrots

Soften gelatin in water. Bring stock to boil, and add gelatin. Stir to dissolve. Add vinegar and lemon juice. Chill to egg-white consistency. Add vegetables, turn into mold, and chill until firm.

Orange Cake

Oven 350°F. 9-inch tube pan, greased and floured.

1 cup softened butter
2 cups sugar
5 eggs
3 cups flour
3 tsp. baking powder
¼ tsp. salt
¾ cup orange juice
grated rind of 1 orange

Cream butter and sugar until light. Beat in eggs one at a time. Sift dry ingredients together. Add to creamed mixture alternately with orange juice. Add orange rind. Bake for 1 hour.

GLAZE

1 cup butter
½ cup sugar
⅓ cup bourbon whiskey or fresh orange juice

Melt butter with sugar and add whiskey or juice. Pour over hot cake. Let cool in pan. Can be frozen.

WRAP A SPECIAL PRESENT LUNCHEON

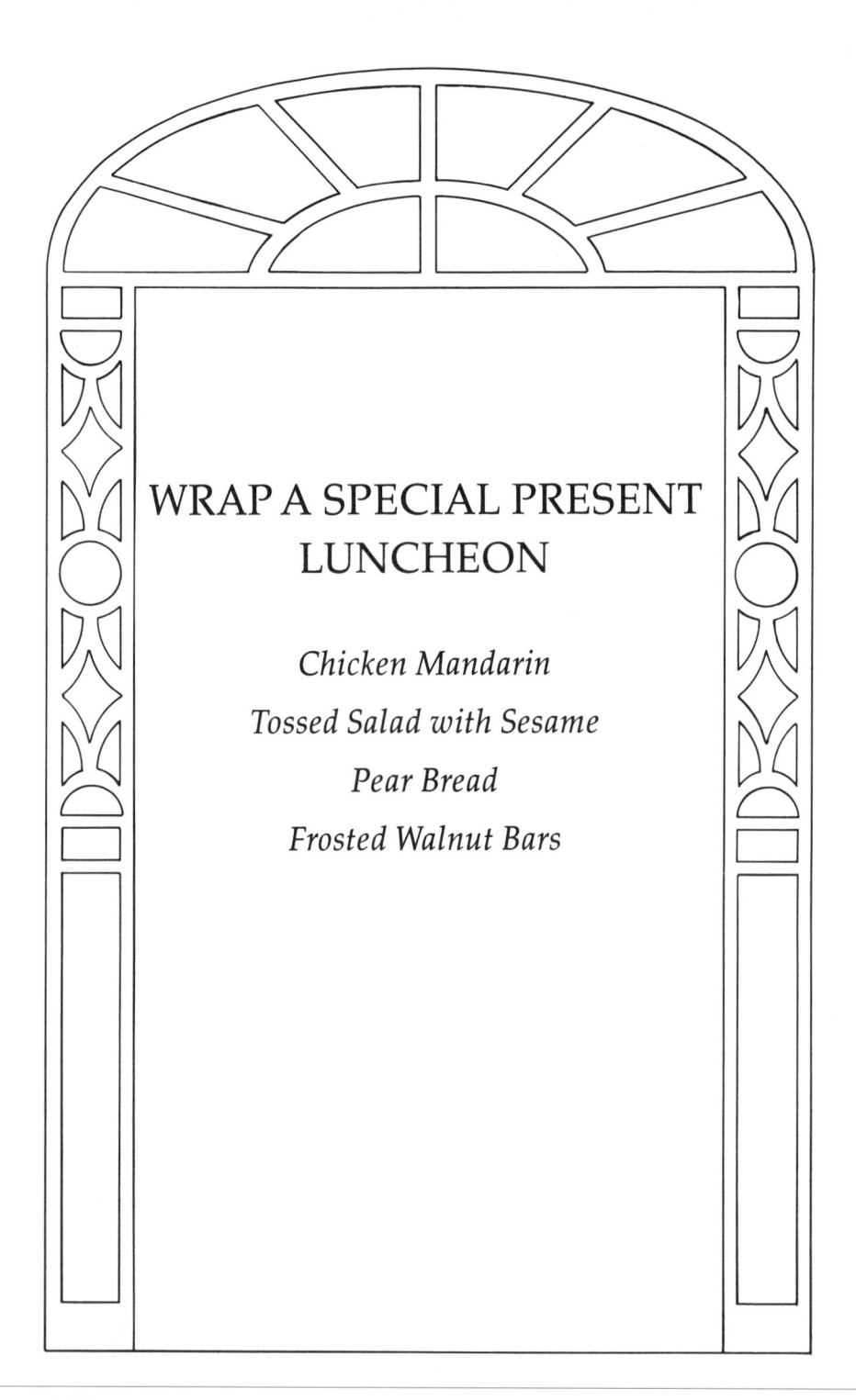

Chicken Mandarin

Tossed Salad with Sesame

Pear Bread

Frosted Walnut Bars

Chicken Mandarin

Serves 8.

¼ lb. butter
⅓ cup cornstarch
3 cups rich chicken stock
1 Tbs. chicken broth concentrate
salt and pepper to taste
2 cups diced cooked chicken
½ cup julienne-cut ham
2 scallions, chopped
¼ cup cooked peas
4-oz. can sliced water chestnuts
½ cup sliced mushrooms, sautéed
4-oz. can mandarin oranges

rice, or chow mein noodles

In skillet melt butter, add cornstarch, and stir until smooth. Add stock, concentrate, salt, and pepper, stirring until thickened.

Add meat and vegetables.

Just before serving add oranges.
Serve with rice or noodles. Freezes well, but do not freeze oranges.

Tossed Salad with Sesame

FRENCH DRESSING
2 cups salad oil, part sesame oil
1 clove garlic, crushed
2 tsp. grated onion
½ tsp. dry mustard
⅛ tsp. pepper
1 tsp. paprika
1 tsp. sugar
½ cup cider vinegar
1 egg white

Beat all dressing ingredients together. Pour onto salad and toss. Sprinkle with toasted sesame seeds.

SALAD
lettuce
escarole
Chinese cabbage
radish roses
sesame seeds, toasted

Pear Bread

Yield 1 loaf. Oven 350°F. 9-inch loaf pan, greased.

½ cup margarine
¾ cup sugar
2 eggs
2 cups flour
½ tsp. salt
1 tsp. baking powder
¼ tsp. nutmeg
¼ cup buttermilk or yogurt
1 cup chopped fresh pears
1 tsp. vanilla

Cream margarine and sugar. Beat in eggs. Sift dry ingredients. Add to creamed mixture alternately with liquid.

Stir in pears and vanilla. Bake for 1 hour.

Frosted Walnut Bars

Oven 350°F. 9x13-inch pan, greased.

CRUST

½ cup margarine
1 cup flour

Work margarine and flour together, and press into pan. Bake for 12 minutes.

FILLING

1 cup walnuts
1½ cups brown sugar
2 Tbs. flour
2 eggs
¼ tsp. baking powder

Chop nuts in blender. Mix with other filling ingredients, and pour over baked crust. Bake 20-25 minutes.

FROSTING

2 Tbs. butter
1 Tbs. lemon juice
1 Tbs. orange juice
1 cup confectioners' sugar

Frost when cool and cut into 1-inch squares.

HOLIDAY COCKTAIL PARTY

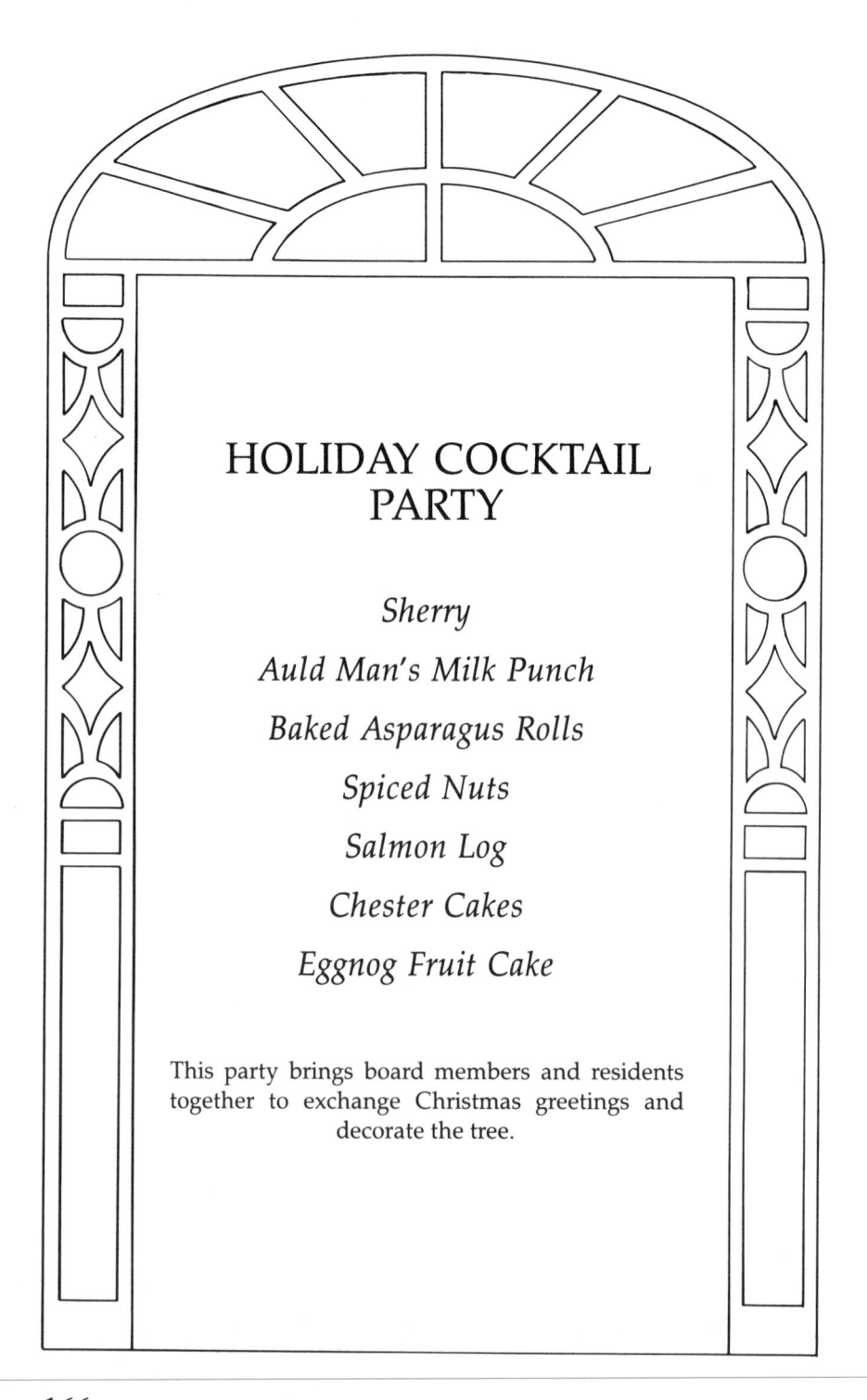

Sherry

Auld Man's Milk Punch

Baked Asparagus Rolls

Spiced Nuts

Salmon Log

Chester Cakes

Eggnog Fruit Cake

This party brings board members and residents together to exchange Christmas greetings and decorate the tree.

Auld Man's Milk Punch

6 eggs, separated
1 cup sugar
1 quart milk or thin cream
½ pint brandy, rum, or whiskey
grated nutmeg

Beat yolks with sugar and add milk. Beat in spirits gradually. Pour into punch bowl. Beat egg whites until stiff. Fold in gently. Sprinkle with nutmeg.

Baked Asparagus Rolls

Oven 350°F.

2 loaves white bread
6 oz. blue cheese
8 oz. cream cheese
1 Tbs. mayonnaise
1 egg, beaten
2 cans asparagus
melted butter

Remove crusts from bread, and roll slices thin. Mix cheeses, mayonnaise, and egg together, and spread on bread slices. Place 1 asparagus spear on each slice, then roll up. Cut into 3 pieces. Dip in melted butter and bake on shallow tray for 15 minutes. Can be frozen before baking.

Spiced Nuts

Oven 375°F. Shallow pan.

¼ cup butter
½ tsp. Tabasco
1 tsp. Worcestershire sauce
1 Tbs. garlic salt
2 cups nut meats

Melt butter in baking pan. Add seasonings. Stir in nuts. Bake for 20-30 minutes. Stir once while baking. Drain on brown paper.

Salmon Log

1-lb can salmon 8 oz. cream cheese, softened 1 Tbs. lemon juice 2 Tbs. grated onion 1 Tbs. Worcestershire sauce 1 tsp. prepared horseradish	Drain and flake salmon, removing skin and bones. Combine with cheese and seasonings and mix well. Chill several hours.
½ cup chopped pecans 3 Tbs. minced parsley	Combine nuts and parsley. Shape salmon into log, and roll in nut mixture. Chill. Serve with crackers.

Chester Cakes

Oven 400-425°F.

¼ lb. sharp Cheddar, grated ¼ lb. margarine 2 cups flour ⅛ tsp. nutmeg ¼ tsp. paprika ¼ tsp. salt 2-4 Tbs. cream 2¼-oz. can devilled ham	Blend cheese and margarine. Mix dry ingredients with cheese mixture. Add cream until dough holds together. Roll to ¼ inch on well-floured board. Cut into rounds. Spread one round with devilled ham; top with another. Push down edges to hold together. Bake for 15 minutes. Serve hot.

Eggnog Fruit Cake

Oven 300°F. Two 9-inch loaf pans, lined with greased wax paper.

2 cups chopped glacé fruits
½ cup chopped walnuts
½ cup slivered blanched almonds
1 jar (3½ oz.) each: green and red glacé cherries
½ cup golden raisins
¾ tsp. mace
6 Tbs. eggnog
4 eggs, beaten
2½ cups flour
1¼ tsp. baking powder
¾ tsp. salt
1¼ cups sugar
¾ cup butter, melted

Combine ingredients in order. Bake 1 hour and 45 minutes. After baking, remove from pan and cool on rack.

EGGNOG FROSTING

⅓ cup softened butter
1 lb. confectioners' sugar
5 Tbs. eggnog

Beat butter and sugar. Gradually add eggnog until the right consistency to drip on cake.

FIRESIDE SUPPER

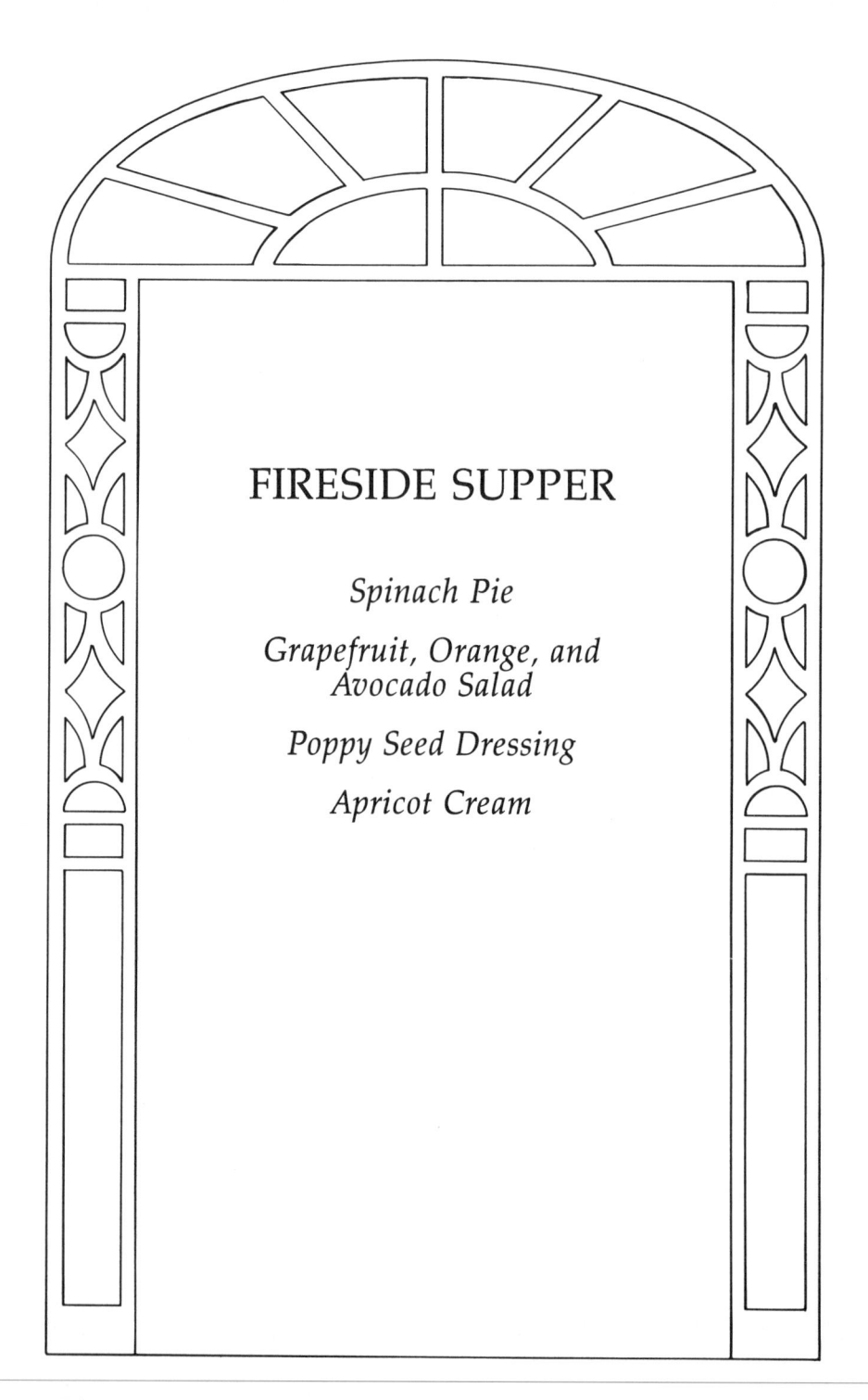

Spinach Pie

Grapefruit, Orange, and Avocado Salad

Poppy Seed Dressing

Apricot Cream

Spinach Pie

Oven 375°F. Two 8-inch pie pans.

CRUST

2 cups whole wheat bread crumbs
½ cup toasted wheat germ
1 cup finely chopped walnuts
½ cup margarine

Mix crust ingredients. Press mixture into pie pans. Bake for 10 minutes. Cool.

FILLING

three 10-oz. packages frozen spinach
3 eggs
½ cup feta cheese
2 cups cottage cheese
2 scallions
2 Tbs. chopped shallots
1 Tbs. margarine
1 Tbs. oil
¼ tsp. nutmeg
1 cup chopped cooked ham
1 cup grated Swiss or Cheddar cheese

Cook spinach. Drain well. Chop. Beat eggs with cheeses. Sauté scallions and shallots in margarine and oil for a few minutes. Combine all together; add nutmeg and ham.

Pour into pie shells and sprinkle grated cheese on top. Bake at 350°F. for 25 minutes.

Grapefruit, Orange, and Avocado Salad

Serves 6.

SALAD
lettuce, escarole, or chicory
1 grapefruit, peeled and sectioned
2 oranges, peeled and sectioned
2 avocados, peeled, sliced, and dipped in citrus juice

Wash, dry, and chill greens. Mix with fruits and toss with poppy seed dressing.

POPPY SEED DRESSING
¾ cup sugar — or part honey
1 tsp. dry mustard
1 tsp. salt
½ cup vinegar — basil or tarragon
1 Tbs. chopped onion
1½ Tbs. tomato juice

Blend dressing ingredients in a blender.

1 cup salad oil
1½ Tbs. poppy seeds

Very slowly blend in oil. Put poppy seeds in last.

Apricot Cream

Serves 6.

1 lb. dried apricots
(½ tsp. cornstarch)
⅔ cup sugar
juice of ½ lemon
heavy cream

Cook apricots in water just to cover until tender. Put through food mill. Return to stove, and thicken if necessary with cornstarch. Add sugar and lemon. Stir over low heat. Cool. Serve with cream on top.

CAROLLING PARTY

Hot Cider and Apple Jack

Sour Cream Twists

Christmas Casserole Cookies

Krisp Kringles

Honey Cake

Mince Tarts

Cranberry Bread

Sour Cream Twists

Oven 400°F. Cookie sheet, greased.

4 cups flour **1 tsp. salt** **1 cup margarine**	Sift flour and salt. Cut in margarine.
1 package dry yeast **¼ cup warm water**	Soften yeast in warm water.
1 egg and 2 egg yolks **1 cup sour cream** **1 tsp. vanilla**	Beat eggs and yolks until foamy. Add sour cream, vanilla, and yeast. Add dry ingredients and mix. Let rise 2 hours or longer in refrigerator.
1 cup sugar mixed with 1 Tbs. cinnamon	Sprinkle some cinnamon sugar on board. Roll out dough ¼-inch thick. Sprinkle with sugar. Roll and fold 4 corners into center. Sprinkle, roll, and fold 4 times in all. Cut into 1x2-inch strips. Twist and place on cookie sheet. Bake for 10 minutes.

Christmas Casserole Cookies

Oven 350°F. 2-quart casserole, ungreased.

2 eggs **1 cup sugar** **1 cup finely chopped dates** **1 cup coconut** **1 cup finely chopped nuts** **1 tsp. vanilla** **¼ tsp. almond extract** **superfine sugar**	Beat eggs; add sugar and beat well. Blend in other ingredients. Put in casserole and bake for 30 minutes. Remove from oven and beat with wooden spoon while still hot. Cool and form into small balls. Roll balls in superfine sugar.

Krisp Kringles

Oven 325°F. Cookie sheet, ungreased.

1 cup butter, melted **1 cup light brown sugar** **1 cup white sugar** **2 eggs** **2 cups flour** **2 cups quick oats** **2 cups Rice Krispies** **1 cup shredded coconut** **1 tsp. salt** **1 tsp. baking soda** **1 tsp. vanilla** *GARNISH* **red candied fruit**	Mix melted butter with all other ingredients. Roll into small balls. Press flat on cookie sheet. Garnish centers with candied fruit. Bake for 10 minutes.

Honey Cake

Oven 350°F. 9x13-inch glass dish lined with oiled wax paper.

- 4 apples, peeled and cored
- 1½ cups honey
- 2½ cups flour
- 1 heaping tsp. baking soda
- ½ tsp. salt
- 1 tsp. cinnamon
- ½ tsp. ground allspice or cloves
- 4 large eggs
- ¾ cup vegetable oil
- 1 tsp. vanilla
- 1 cup raisins
- 1 cup chopped walnuts

Cook apples with ¾ cup honey until soft. Cool. Sift dry ingredients. Beat eggs with remaining ¾ cup honey, oil, vanilla, and apples. Add remaining ingredients. Mix everything together. Pour into prepared pan. Bake for 20 minutes at 350°F., then for another 20 minutes at 325°F. This is a Russian-Jewish cake that is used for celebrations. It keeps and freezes well.

Mince Tarts

Yield: 18. Oven 425°F. Tartlet pans.

PASTRY

2 cups flour
2 Tbs. sugar
¼ tsp. salt
11 Tbs. shortening (8 Tbs. butter, 3 Tbs. lard)
6 Tbs. water (or enough to make pliable pastry)
mincemeat

confectioner's sugar

Combine pastry ingredients and roll out pastry ⅛ inch thick. Cut into 3-inch rounds. Line pans with pastry. Place 1 tsp. mincemeat in each pastry round. Cover with second pastry round. Crimp edges together; prick tops. Bake for 20 minutes. Serve warm, dusted with confectioners' sugar. If frozen, reheat at 425°F. for about 15 minutes.

Cranberry Bread

Oven 350°F. 9-inch loaf pan, greased.

2 cups sifted flour
1½ cups sugar
1½ tsp. baking powder
½ tsp. baking soda
1 tsp. salt
¼ cup margarine
1 egg, well beaten
¾ cup orange juice
1 Tbs. grated orange rind
1 or 2 cups cranberries

Sift dry ingredients. Cut in margarine. Combine egg, orange juice, and rind. Stir into dry ingredients. Fold in cranberries. Bake about 1 hour.

NEW YEAR'S DAY FÊTE

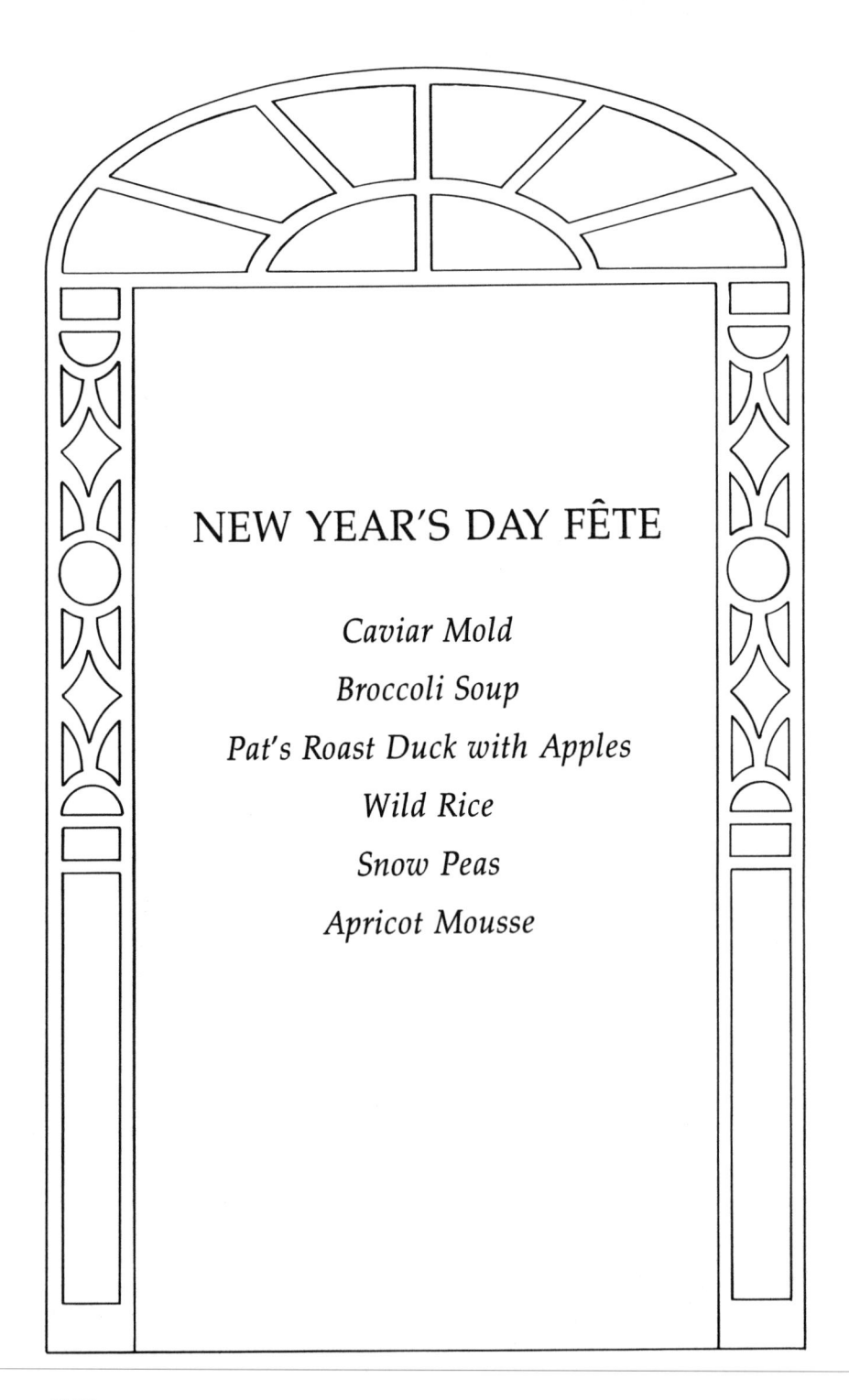

Caviar Mold

Broccoli Soup

Pat's Roast Duck with Apples

Wild Rice

Snow Peas

Apricot Mousse

Caviar Mold

3-cup mold.

1 envelope plain gelatin
4 Tbs. lemon juice
16 oz. sour cream
3 hard-boiled eggs, mashed
1 small onion, finely chopped
3½-oz. jar black caviar

Dissolve gelatin in lemon juice, and stir over low heat until clear. Combine sour cream, eggs, and onion, and add to gelatin. Stir in caviar very lightly. Chill in mold until set. Serve with plain crackers.

Broccoli Soup

Serves 10-12.

3 cups beef stock
1 medium head broccoli, chopped
1 Tbs. fresh tarragon, or 1 tsp. dried
1 tsp. fresh basil
1 tsp. marjoram
1 tsp. thyme
1 pint light cream

⅛ tsp. nutmeg

Cook chopped broccoli in stock with herbs until tender, about 15 minutes. Whirl broccoli in blender with 1 cup of liquid. Return to broth mixture in saucepan. Add cream, but do not boil. (If thickening is desired, make a roux of 3 Tbs. butter and 2 Tbs. flour, stir some soup into it until smooth, then blend with soup in pot.) Sprinkle nutmeg on top of each serving.

Pat's Roast Duck

Oven 450°F.

4-5 lb. duck

STUFFING

6 sour apples, cored, peeled, and chopped
1 cup bread crumbs
½ tsp. poultry seasoning
½ tsp. salt
(few cooked prunes)

Cook apples in water to cover until half done. Drain. Mix with other ingredients. Wipe duck and sprinkle body cavity with salt. Stuff. Prick skin all over. Place on a rack in a baking pan in hot oven and bake for 15 minutes. Then lower oven temperature to 325°F. and bake for 22 minutes per pound.

Apricot Mousse

Serves 12. 10-inch spring-form pan.

8-oz. package dried apricots
¼ cup Grand Marnier
20 lady fingers, split
two 8-oz. packages cream cheese, softened
1 cup brown sugar
4 egg yolks
1 tsp. almond extract
4 egg whites
¼ tsp. salt
½ cup brown sugar
2 cups heavy cream, whipped

Cook apricots in just enough water to cover until soft. Puree in blender with cooking water and Grand Marnier. Dry split lady fingers in 200°F. oven for 10 minutes. Cool. Line pan with lady fingers, cut sides facing inward. Beat cream cheese with 1 cup brown sugar, adding yolks one at a time. Stir in apricot mixture and almond extract. Beat whites with salt until stiff and gradually add ½ cup brown sugar. Fold whipped cream and egg whites into apricot mixture. Pour into pan and refrigerate at least 8 hours before serving.

GARNISH
fresh fruit

Garnish as suggested.

SUPPER AND SING-ALONG

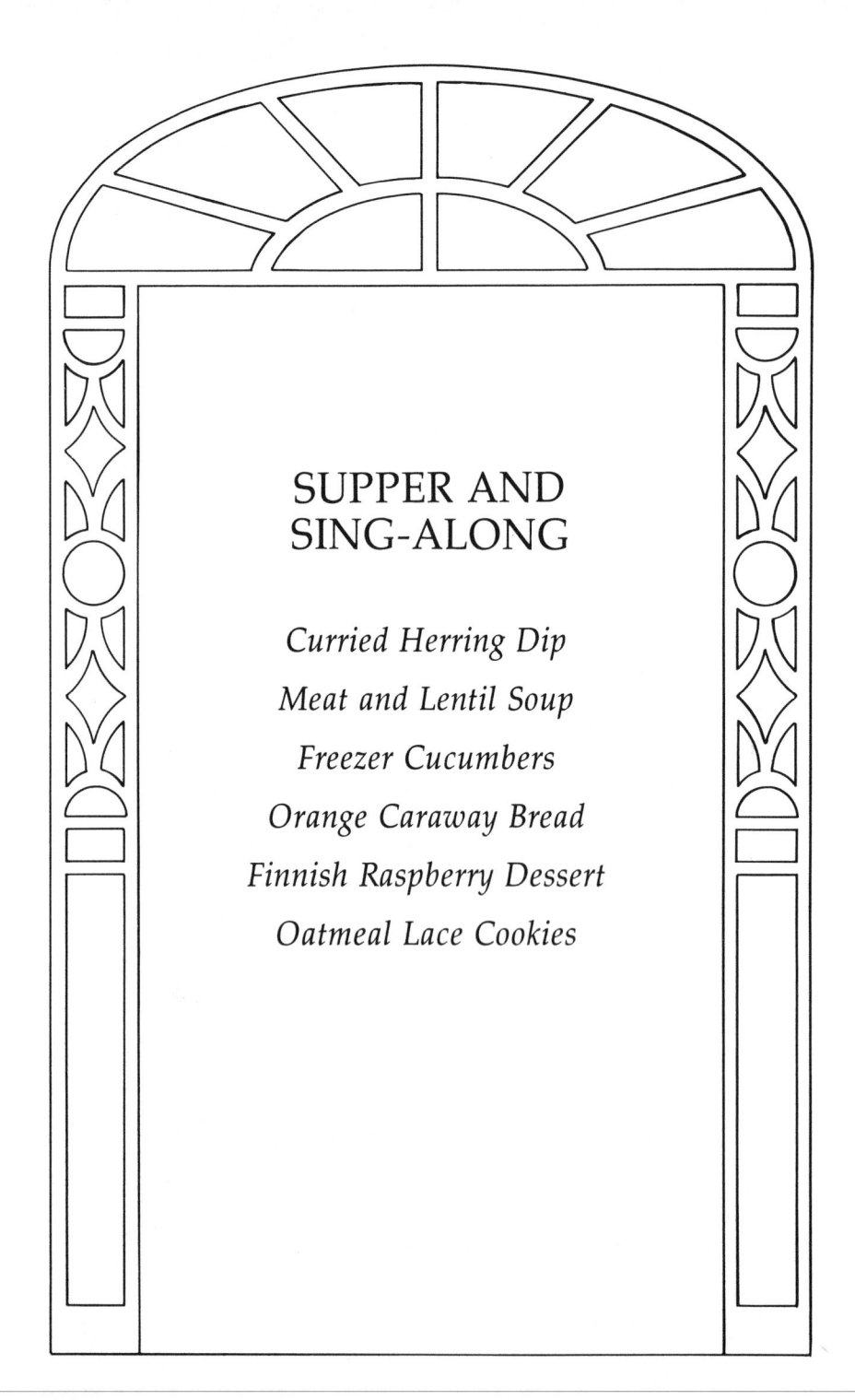

Curried Herring Dip

Meat and Lentil Soup

Freezer Cucumbers

Orange Caraway Bread

Finnish Raspberry Dessert

Oatmeal Lace Cookies

Curried Herring Dip

1½ cups marinated herring, drained
¾ cup mayonnaise
1 tsp. curry powder
¼ tsp. ground turmeric
⅛ tsp. ground coriander
dash ground cinnamon

Mix all ingredients. Cover and chill at least 2 hours, or up to 5 days.

Serve with rye bread and butter.

Meat and Lentil Soup

1 lb. lean lamb
8 cups water
salt and pepper
1 cup dried lentils
2 potatoes, peeled and cubed
2 Tbs. melted butter
½ cup dried prunes or apricots
ground cumin
ground coriander

Simmer meat in water in large pot with salt and pepper for 1 hour. Skim off foam. Stir in lentils and cook ½ hour. Sauté potatoes in butter in skillet, browning evenly. Add to soup with fruit, and simmer 30 minutes more. Season with spices to taste.

CONDIMENTS

1 pint yogurt mixed with 2 cloves garlic, pressed
walnuts, chopped
lemon or lime wedges

Serve with condiments.

Freezer Cucumbers

4 cucumbers, sliced thinly
1 medium onion, sliced
2 tsp. salt
2 cups sugar
¾ cup vinegar

Place cucumbers, onion, and salt in bowl, and let stand 2 hours. Drain well. Heat sugar and vinegar, but do *not* boil. Cool. Pour over cucumbers. Seal in plastic bags or boxes. Freeze until needed. Thaw 1 hour. They do retain their crispness!

Orange Caraway Bread

Yield: 2 loaves. Oven 375°F.

1 Tbs. sugar
½ cup water
1 cup milk
½ cup molasses
¼ cup shortening
2 packages yeast
1½ Tbs. caraway seeds
2 Tbs. grated orange rind
1 egg, beaten
2 cups rye flour
2 cups white flour, plus more for kneading
corn meal

Heat in saucepan: sugar, water, milk, molasses, and shortening. Cool to lukewarm. Add yeast, caraway, and orange rind. Put in large mixer bowl, and add egg. Beat in rye flour, then white flour. This is a sticky dough, best kneaded in mixer. Let rise in greased, covered bowl about 2 hours. Punch down, knead lightly on floured board, and shape into loaves. Sprinkle corn meal on greased loaf pans. Let rise until double, about 1 hour. Bake for 20-25 minutes or until cake tester comes out clean.

Finnish Raspberry Dessert

3-oz. package raspberry gelatin
1 cup boiling water
10-oz. package frozen raspberries
2 cups applesauce
sour cream for topping

Add gelatin to boiling water and stir in frozen berries. Stir until thawed. Add applesauce. Refrigerate at least 2 hours. Serve with dollop of sour cream on top.

Oatmeal Lace Cookies

Oven 350°F. Cookie sheets covered with foil, dull side up.

¼ lb. butter, melted
1 cup sugar
1 egg
1 cup *quick* oatmeal
1 Tbs. flour
1 tsp. vanilla
½ tsp. salt

Mix all ingredients and drop on cookie sheets in very small amounts — about ½ tsp. Bake 6-8 minutes. Watch carefully. They should be brown around edges, but are easy to overdo. Cool on baking sheet. Peel off foil and store in covered jar.

HOME FROM THE HOSPITAL

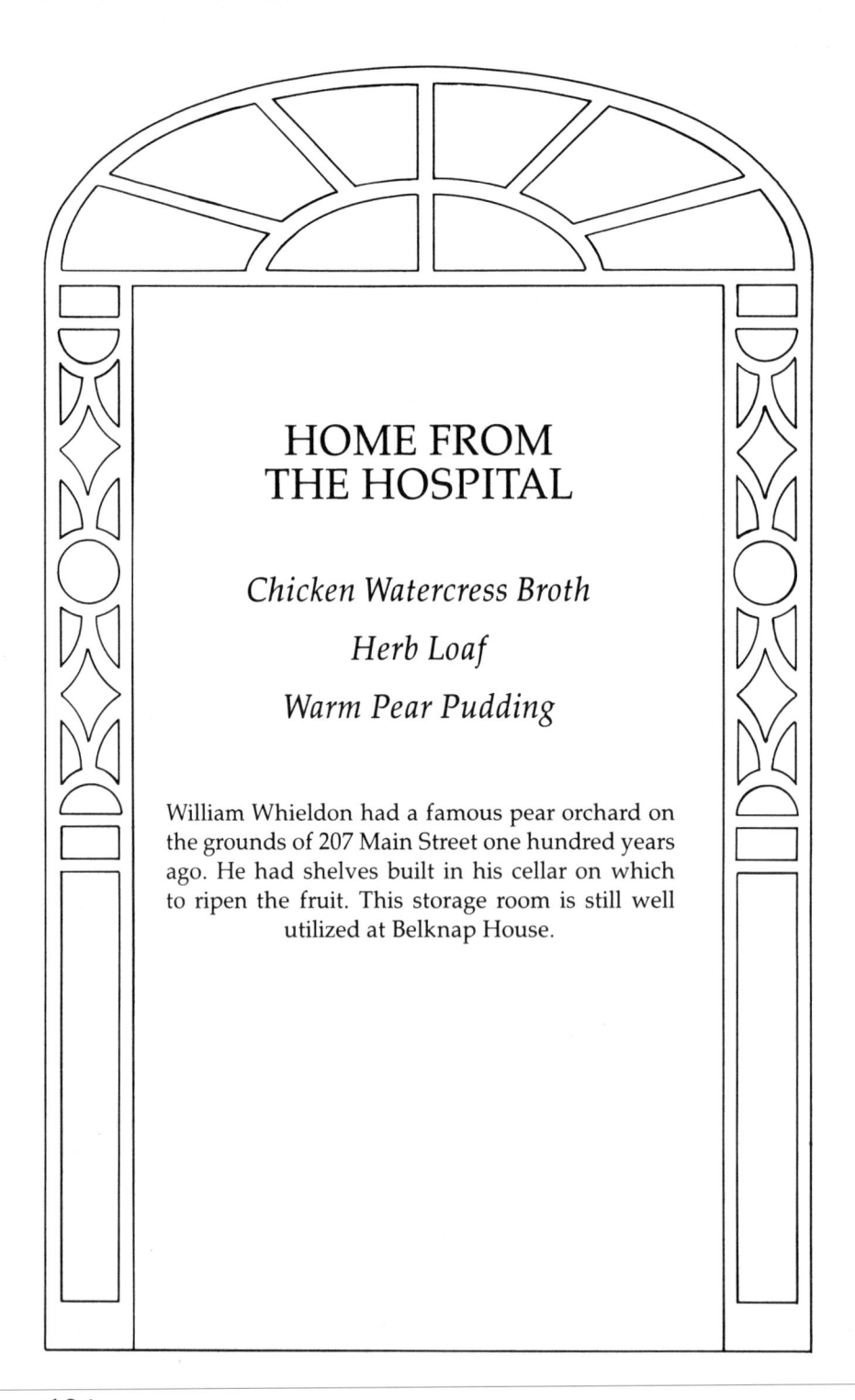

Chicken Watercress Broth

Herb Loaf

Warm Pear Pudding

William Whieldon had a famous pear orchard on the grounds of 207 Main Street one hundred years ago. He had shelves built in his cellar on which to ripen the fruit. This storage room is still well utilized at Belknap House.

Chicken Watercress Broth

1 bunch watercress
2 Tbs. butter
2 cups chicken stock
1 egg

Chop watercress, and sauté in butter for 3 minutes in saucepan. Add chicken stock and heat. Beat egg with fork, and add to hot soup, beating with whisk.

Herb Loaf

Oven 450°F.

4 oz. butter
1 Tbs. mixed herbs
juice of ¼ lemon
freshly ground black pepper
½ clove garlic, crushed
1 loaf French bread

Cream butter with other ingredients. Cut loaf into ½-inch slices. Spread both sides of each slice with butter mixture. Wrap loaf in foil and bake. After 10 minutes, reduce heat to 375°F., and open foil for 10 minutes. Serve hot.

Warm Pear Pudding

Oven 325°F.

2 large pears, peeled and sliced
1½ Tbs. melted butter
½ tsp. nutmeg
2 eggs
¼ cup brown sugar
1½ cups milk
¼ tsp. almond or vanilla extract

Place pear slices in baking dish, pour butter over pears, and sprinkle with nutmeg. Beat eggs with other ingredients and pour over pears. Place baking dish in larger pan filled with hot water. Bake for 45 minutes.

VALENTINE DINNER

Artichoke Hearts Vinaigrette

Roast Stuffed Pork

Roast Potatoes

Baked Onions with Spinach

Cranberry Velvet Pie

Artichoke Hearts Vinaigrette

two 8½-oz. cans artichoke hearts, drained

DRESSING
4 Tbs. olive oil
2 Tbs. white-wine vinegar
2 tsp. Dijon mustard
1 Tbs. chopped shallots
½ tsp. salt
¼ tsp. pepper

lettuce
1 Tbs. chopped parsley
2 tsp. chopped tarragon

Marinate artichoke hearts in dressing for several hours. When ready to serve, drain artichokes, place on lettuce leaves, and sprinkle with parsley and tarragon.

Roast Stuffed Pork

Serves 6. Oven 325°F.

5-6 lb. pork loin
½ tsp. salt
½ tsp. cinnamon
½ tsp. allspice
½ tsp. pepper
¼ tsp. cloves
12 pitted prunes
2 apples, cored, peeled, and chopped
1 cup chopped dried apricots
¼ tsp. cinnamon
cider, or apple juice

Have bone sawed through. Make 2 pockets in meat parallel to bone. Combine seasonings and rub on meat.

Cook fruits until soft. Add cinnamon. Stuff fruits into pockets, wrap and tie. Roast 30 minutes per pound. Baste with cider or apple juice. Serve with roast potatoes.

Baked Onions with Spinach

Serves 6. Oven 350°F.

MORNAY SAUCE

3 Tbs. butter
3 Tbs. flour
1 cup milk
¼ cup cream
¼ cup grated Gruyère cheese
dash of salt, pepper, nutmeg

Melt butter and stir in flour. Gradually add milk and cream and stir until thickened. Add cheese and seasonings.

ONIONS

6 large mild onions
two 10-oz. packages frozen chopped spinach, cooked and drained
4 Tbs. butter, melted

TOPPING

bread crumbs
additonal grated Gruyère cheese
2 Tbs. butter

Peel onions. Steam 30 minutes. Drain and cool. Take out centers to make cups. Puree centers with spinach. Add butter and sauce. Stuff onions with this mixture, and top with bread crumbs and grated cheese. Dot with butter. Place onions with small amount of stock or water in baking dish. Cover. Bake 45 minutes. Uncover for last 15 minutes.

Cranberry Velvet Pie

Oven 375°F. 9-inch pie plate, greased.

CRUST

16 graham-cracker squares
6 Tbs. melted margarine
½ cup sugar

Roll crackers into fine crumbs. Combine ingredients. Press ⅔ mixture in pie plate to make shell. Bake for 8 minutes. Cool.

FILLING

1 Tbs. plain gelatin
½ cup orange juice
8 oz. cream cheese, softened
1 cup whipping cream
½ cup confectioners' sugar
½ tsp. vanilla
1-lb. can whole cranberry sauce

Soften gelatin in ¼ cup juice. Heat remaining juice. Add to gelatin, stirring until dissolved. Beat cheese until fluffy and gradually add gelatin mixture. Whip cream with sugar and vanilla until stiff. Fold, along with cranberry sauce, into cheese mixture. Spoon into crust and chill for at least 3 hours.

GARNISH

remaining crumb mixture
whipped cream

At serving time, garnish as suggested.

COLD WINTER'S NIGHT SUPPER

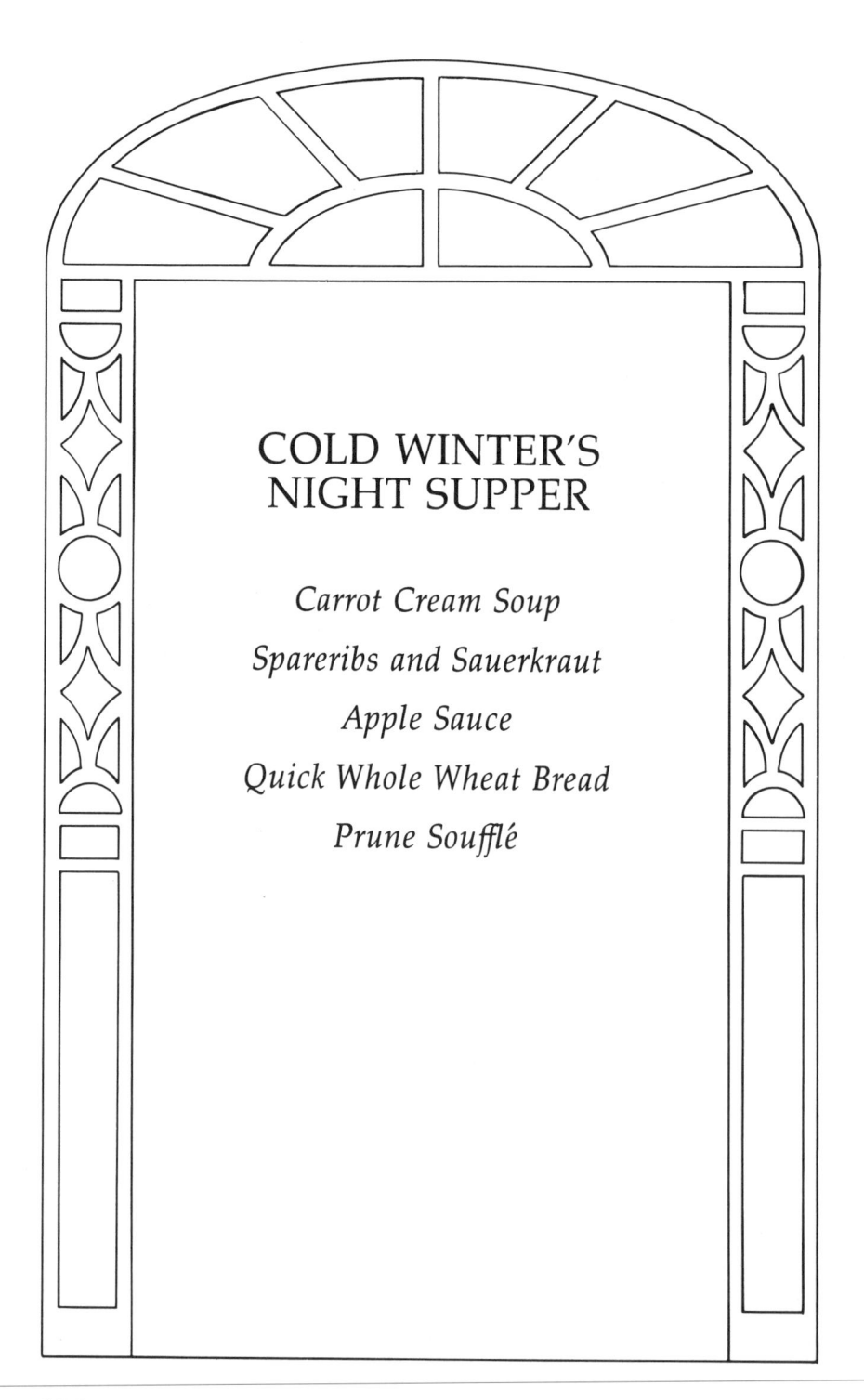

Carrot Cream Soup

Spareribs and Sauerkraut

Apple Sauce

Quick Whole Wheat Bread

Prune Soufflé

Carrot Cream Soup

Serves 6.

- 4-5 cups sliced carrots
- ¼ cup chopped onion
- ½ tsp. sugar
- ½ tsp. marjoram
- ¼ tsp. thyme
- 2-3 Tbs. butter, or chicken fat
- ¼ cup raw brown rice
- 2 cups milk
- 1 bay leaf
- 4 cups vegetable or chicken stock
- ½ cup heavy cream
- salt

GARNISH
- chopped fresh mint, or chervil
- grated carrot, or watercress

Cook first 5 ingredients in butter until vegetables are slightly soft. Stir in rice to coat. Brown slightly. Add milk, bay leaf, and 1 cup of stock. Simmer 30 minutes. Discard bay leaf. Puree in blender. Add remaining stock and cream. Salt to taste. Reheat, but do not boil.

Garnish as suggested. May also be served cold.

Percy Thyng's Spareribs and Sauerkraut

Serves 6.

- 3 Tbs. shortening
- 4 lbs. spareribs
- two 1-lb cans sauerkraut
- 1 Tbs. brown sugar
- 1 cup water
- 6 potatoes, peeled and halved

Put shortening in pot and heat until it sizzles. Brown ribs on all sides. Put sauerkraut in strainer, and rinse in cold water. Add to pot. Sprinkle all with brown sugar; add water. Cook slowly for 1½ hours. Add potatoes and cook for ½ hour more.

Quick Whole Wheat Bread

Yield: 1 loaf. Oven 325°F. 9-inch loaf pan, greased.

1 cup white flour **2 cups whole wheat flour** **½ cup sugar** **1 tsp. salt** **1 tsp. baking soda** **1½ cups milk** **½ cup molasses**	Sift dry ingredients together. Stir in liquids and mix well. Put in pan, and bake for 1½ hours. Cool. Wrap in foil, and store in refrigerator. Slice thinly to serve. It is very good toasted.

Prune Soufflé

Serves 6. Oven 375°F. 1-quart soufflé dish, greased.

1 lb. prunes **2 cups water to cover** **4 egg whites** **1 cup sugar** **1 Tbs. lemon juice** **1 tsp. vanilla** **¼ cup sherry** **whipped cream**	Cook prunes in water until soft, drain, pit, and puree. Beat egg whites until stiff, slowly beating in sugar and lemon juice. Fold in pureed prunes, vanilla, and sherry. Pour into dish. Set baking dish in pan with water reaching ¼ up sides of dish. Bake for 45 minutes. Serve with whipped cream. May be served warm or cold.

BIRTHDAY DINNER

Hot Hors d'Oeuvre Spread

Artichoke Hearts with Spinach

Chicken Breasts Grand Marnier

Carrots Malaga

Chocolate Zucchini Cake

Hot Hors D'Oeuvre Spread

10-oz. jar pineapple preserves
10-oz. jar apple jelly
2-oz. jar prepared horseradish
1 Tbs. dry mustard
black pepper
crackers
cream cheese, softened

Mix together, spoon into jars, and store in refrigerator. ("Hot" in the title refers to the taste.)

Serve with crackers spread with cream cheese.

Artichoke Hearts and Spinach

Oven 350°F.

three 10-oz. packages frozen chopped spinach
salt and dash pepper
dash nutmeg
¾ cup heavy cream
two 8½-oz. cans artichoke hearts, drained
1 onion, chopped
1 Tbs. unsalted butter
1 cup grated Swiss cheese

Cook spinach, drain, and season. Mix with cream. Halve artichoke hearts, and briefly sauté with onion in melted butter. Place artichokes and onion in shallow baking dish. Top with creamed spinach. Sprinkle with cheese. Bake for 20 minutes, or until browned.

Chicken Breasts Grand Marnier

Serves 6. Oven 350°F.

3 chicken breasts, halved
seasoned flour
¼ cup butter
¼ tsp. dried rosemary
2 shallots, chopped finely
½ cup minced onion
1 cup orange juice
½ cup Grand Marnier
2 oranges, thinly sliced

Coat chicken breasts with flour, and brown in butter. Put in casserole and sprinkle with rosemary and shallots. Sauté onion in butter, and add to it the orange juice and Grand Marnier. Bring to boil, and pour over chicken. Cut orange slices in half and lay over chicken. Bake for 1 hour.

Carrots Malaga

Serves 6-8.

2 lbs. carrots, cut in thick diagonal slices
margarine or butter
⅛ tsp. sugar
1 Tbs. vodka
½ cup water
1 cup Malaga grapes, sliced or whole
salt and pepper

Sauté carrots in butter for a few minutes. Stir in sugar, then vodka and water. Simmer tightly covered, until almost tender. Add grapes, and cook until carrots are tender. Season with salt and pepper.

Chocolate Zucchini Cake

Oven 350°F. Bundt pan, greased and floured, or two 7-inch loaf pans, greased and floured.

2½ cups flour
½ cup cocoa
2½ tsp. baking powder
1½ tsp. baking soda
1 tsp. salt
1 tsp. cinnamon
¾ cup margarine
2 cups sugar
3 eggs
2 tsp. vanilla
2 cups coarsely grated zucchini, loosely measured
½ cup milk
1 cup chopped nuts

Sift dry ingredients together. Cream margarine and sugar. Beat in eggs and vanilla. Stir in zucchini with a spoon. Add dry ingredients alternately with milk, using spoon. Add nuts. Bake 30 minutes to 1 hour, depending on pan size. Cool in pan 15 minutes, then turn out on rack. Cover cake and store for a few days, as this cake becomes more moist as it matures. Make two at a time and freeze one.

GLAZE

2 cups confectioners' sugar
3 Tbs. milk
1 tsp. vanilla

Drizzle glaze on cake just before serving. A wonderful treat in winter.

The drawings in this book are scenes from Belknap House, 207 Main Street, Concord, Massachusetts.

INDEX

A
Almond Lemon Cake 31
Almond Spread, Chicken 104
Angel Food Cake, Filled 96
Antipasto Salad 51
APPETIZERS
   Artichoke Hearts Vinaigrette 189
   Artichoke Squares 1
   Asparagus Rolls, Baked 167
   Baba Ghanouj 137
   Bean Pâté, White 148
   Beef Dip, Smoked 116
   Caviar Mold 179
   Cheese Crispies 155
   Chester Cakes 168
   Chicken Almond Spread 104
   Cottage Cheese Dip 54
   Crabmeat Dip, Hot 148
   Cucumber Boats 54
   Cucumber Dip 81
   Curry Dip, Vegetable 98
   Eggs, Stuffed 29
   Eggplant Spread, Baked 111
      and Pine Nut Dip 95
   Garden Crispies 71
   Herring Dip, Curried 183
   Hot Hors d'Oeuvre Spread 196
   Liver Pâté, Danish 19
   Mayonnaise Dip, Green 143
   Mushrooms, Stuffed 103
   Nuts, Spiced 167
   Salmon Log 168
   Spinach Squares 147
   Sugar Snap Peas, Blue Cheese 90
Apple Cake 123
   Pie, New England 100
   Stuffing 180
Apricot Cream 172
   Ice Cream 109
   Mousse 181
Artichoke Hearts Vinaigrette 189
   and Spinach 196
   Squares 1
Asparagus and Ham Rolls 30
   Baked 167
   in Puff Pastry 43
   Soup 5
Aspic, Tomato 155
Auld Man's Milk Punch 167

B
Baba Ghanouj 137
Basil Jelly 2
Beans, Marinated Green 61
Bean Pâté, White 148
Beef Bourguignon 112
   Chuck Roast, Marinated 82
   Hamburgers, Special 108
   Spiced Curried 37
   Warm Smoked, and Cheese Dip 116
Beet and Celery Mold, Jellied 16
   and Rice Salad 99
BEVERAGES: See DRINKS
Biscuits, Orange 92
Blackberries, Peaches with 73
Blueberry Muffins 83
Blueberries, Red, White and 57
Bran-Buttermilk Muffins 118
   Carrot-, Muffins 91
Brandade Fish Salad 59
Brandy Ice Cream 76
BREADSTUFFS
   Blueberry Muffins 83
   Bran-Buttermilk Muffins 118
   Brioche 48
   Carrot-Bran Muffins 91
   Cheesy Cornbread 12
   Cranberry Bread 177
   Currant Buns 105
      Scones 140
   Dill Muffins 14
   English Muffin Bread 24
   French Bread, No-Knead 63
      Quick 113
   Herb Batter Bread 30
      Bread 132
      Loaf 187
   Lemon Bread 133
   Oatmeal Scones 129
   Onion Cornbread Muffins 131
   Orange Biscuits 72
      Caraway Bread 184
   Pappadums 37
   Pear Bread 164
   Popovers 34
   Poppy Seed Muffins 121
   Refrigerator Rolls 68
   Scones, Currant 140
      Oatmeal 129

Sour Cream Twists 174
Sour Dough Bread 21
    Bread Sticks 7
    Date Raisin Coffee Bread 41
    Starter 6
    Streusel Coffee Cake 40
Syrian Bread 60
Three-Grain Bread 134
Tritical Bread 83
Whole Wheat Bread, Quick 194
Yorkshire Pudding 156
Zucchini Bread 99
Brioche 48
Broccoli Salad 121
    Soup 179
Brussels Sprouts with Chestnuts 157
Buttermilk Dressing 82

C
CAKES
    Almond Lemon 31
    Angel Food, Filled 96
    Apple, Osgood Williams' 123
    Cardamom 8
    Chestnut Gâteau 145
    Chocolate Zucchini 198
    Eggnog Fruit 169
    Honey 176
    Orange 161
    Plum 157
    Poppy Seed 35
    Pumpkin Fruit 141
Cantaloupe Ice 92
    Shells, Turkey Salad in 33
Caraway Orange Bread 184
Cardamon Cake 8
Carrot-Bran Muffins 91
Carrot Casserole 6
    Malaga 197
    Soup, Cream 193
    Tomato 14
Casserole Cookies, Christmas 175
CASSEROLES
    Beef Bourguignon 112
    Carrot 6
    Swiss Eggs 40
    Leeks with Ham 47
    Pasta al Forno 20
    Peppers, Grandmother's 134
Caviar Mold 179
Champagne Strawberry Punch 103
Cheese Cake 61
    Chocolate 152
    Crispies 155
Cheesy Cornbread 12

Chester Cakes 168
Chestnut Gâteau 145
Chestnuts, Brussels Sprouts with 157
Chicken Almond Spread 104
    Breasts Grand Marnier 197
    Cold Lemon 90
    Curry, Mellow 71
    Mandarin 163
    Livers 159
    Sandwiches 133
    Spicy Sauce for Grilled 98
    Watercress Broth 187
Chocolate Cheese Cake 152
    Chocolate Chips 78
    Colonial Pie 17
    Mousse, White 106
    Orange Bars 52
    Shot Cookies 141
    Zucchini Cake 198
Chuck Roast, Marinated 82
Citrus Marmalade 25
Clam Chowder 10
Coffee Bar 41
    Kisses 77
Colonial Pie 17
Coleslaw with Fruit 63
COOKIES
    Butter, Corn-Meal 49
    Casserole, Christmas 175
    Chocolate Chocolate Chips 78
        Orange Bars 52
        Shot 141
    Coffee Kisses 77
    Corn-Meal Butter 49
    Fennel 93
    Ginger 73
    Ginger, Swedish 44
    Graham Cracker Praline 87
    High-Energy Bars 111
    Krisp Kringles 175
    Oatmeal Lace 185
    Raisin, Low-Sodium 88
    Shortbread 27
    Shrewsbury Biscuits 79
    Toffee Bars 127
    Vanilla 77
    Walnut Bars, Frosted 165
    Zucchini Drop 87
Cornish Game Hens 117
Cornbread, Cheesy 12
    Muffins 131
Corn-Meal Butter Cookies 49
Cottage Cheese Dip 54
Crabmeat Dip, Hot 148

Cranberry Borscht 143
  Bread 177
  Pudding, Steamed 118
  Tea, Spiced 140
  Velvet Pie 191
Crispies, Cheese 155
  Garden 71
Cucumber Dip 81
  Raita 38
  Slices, Stuffed 54
Cucumbers, Tomatoes stuffed with 117
  Freezer 184
Currant Buns 105
  Scones 140
Curried Herring Dip 98
Curry, Chicken 71
  Dip, Vegetable 98
  Herring Dip 183
  Soup, Cold 33

D
DESSERTS
  Apricot Cream 172
    Mousse 181
  Cheese Cake 61
    Chocolate 152
  Chocolate Mousse, White 106
  Cranberry Pudding, Steamed 118
  Finnish Raspberry 185
  Fruit
    Blueberries, Red, White and 57
    Grapes in Drambuie Sauce 43
    Fruit Kebabs 131
    Macedoine 120
    Strawberries 27
  Ginger Roll, Almond 3
  Ice Cream
    Apricot, Easiest 109
    Brandy 76
    Vanilla 75
  Ices, Fruit 92
  Lemon Pudding 38
  Lemon Soufflé, Cold 22
  Mocha Mousse 138
  Pancake, Swedish 135
  Pavlova 151
  Peaches in Wine Gelatin 8
  Pear Pudding 187
  Pears with Mint Sorbet 127
  Pie
    Apple, New England 100
    Colonial 17
    Cranberry Velvet 191
    Lemon Fluff 65
    Mince Tarts 177

Pineapple-Mint Fantasy 84
Prune Soufflé 194
Pudding, Steamed Cranberry 118
  Lemon 38
  Pear 187
Pumpkin Roll 114
Raspberry Dessert, Finnish 185
Rhubarb Swirl 12
Sherbert, Strawberry 76
Sorbet, Pears with Mint 127
Soufflé, Cold Lemon 22
  Prune 194
Sour Cream, Dessert, Gertrude Fallon's 69
Dill Muffins 14
DRINKS
  Champagne Punch 103
  Coffee Bar 41
  Milk Punch, Auld Man's 167
  Rhine Wine Cooler 24
  Rhubarb Punch 29
  Rosy Punch 120
  Shandy 81
  Spritzer 47
  Tea, Cranberry, Spiced 140
    Iced, Eleanor Fenn's 86
Duck, Pat's Roast, with Apples 180

E
Egg Sauce 55
Eggs, Stuffed 29
  Swiss 40
Eggnog Fruit Cake 169
Eggplant, Baba Ghanouj 137
  Dip 95
  Spread, Baked 111
English Muffin Loaf 24

F
Fantasy, Pineapple-Mint 84
Fennel Cookies 93
FISH
  Brandade Salad 59
  Fishball Chowder 64
  Salmon, Poached 55
  Schrod, Mustard Sauce 11
  Seafood Newburg 104
  Shrimp Gumbo on Rice 130
  Soup, Oriental 149
  Soused 67
French Bread, No-Knead 63
  Quick 113
French Dressing 164
FRUIT
  Blackberries, Peaches with 73
  Blueberries, Red, White and 57

Cake, Eggnog 169
Grapes in Drambuie Sauce 43
Ices 92
Kebabs 131
Macedoine 120
Peaches with Blackberries 73
Strawberries 27

G
Garden Crispies 71
   Salad 91
Ginger Almond Roll 3
   Cookies 73, Swedish 44
Graham Cracker Praline Cookies 87
Grandmother's Peppers 134
Grapefruit, Orange, and Avocado Salad 172
Grapes in Drambuie Sauce 43
   with Carrots 197
Green Garden Salad 91
   Dressing 91
   Salad 22
   Vegetable Platter 105
Greens, Mixed Salad 130
   Tossed with Sesame 164
Grits Soufflé 1

H
Ham Rolls, Asparagus and 30
   Leeks with, in Dill Sauce 47
Hamburgers, Special 108
Herb Batter Bread 30
Herb Bread 132
Herb Loaf 187
Herring and Macaroni Salad 81
   Dip, Curried 183
High-Energy Bars 111
Honey Cake 176
Honeydew Melon with Fruit Ices 92
Hot Hors d'Oeuvre Spread 196

I
Ice Cream, Apricot 109
   Brandy 76
   Vanilla 75
Iced Tea, Eleanor Fenn's 86

J
Jelly, Basil 2

K
Krisp Kringles 175

L
Lamb Steak, Grilled 2
   and Pear Stew 137

Leeks with Ham in Dill Sauce 47
Lemon Bread 133
   Chicken, Cold 90
   Fluff Pie 65
   Pudding 38
   Soufflé, Cold 22
Lentil Soup, Meat and 183
Livers, Chicken 159
Liver Pâté, Danish 19

M
Macaroni Salad, Herring and 81
Macedoine Salad 5
Marmalade, Citrus 25
Mayonnaise Dip, Green 143
Meat and Lentil Soup 183
Melon, Honeydew 92
Mince Tarts 177
Mint Fantasy, Pineapple- 84
   Sorbet 127
Mocha Mousse 138
Mushroom and Watercress Sandwich Filling 132
Mushrooms, Scallops and 125
   Stuffed 103
Mustard Sauce 15

N
New England Apple Pie 100
Nutty Spaghetti 108
Nuts, Spiced 167

O
Oatmeal Lace Cookies 185
   Scones 129
Onion and Black Olive Salad, Orange 149
   Baked with Spinach 190
   Cornbread Muffins 131
   Pie 160
Orange Biscuits 72
   Cake 161
   Caraway Bread 184
   Onion, and Black Olive Salad 149
Oriental Fish Soup 149
Oriental Salad 126
Oysters, Creamed Turkey and 144

P
Pancake, Swedish 135
Pappadums 37
Paprika Dressing 69
Pasta al Forno 20
Pâté, Danish Liver 19
Pavlova 151

Peaches with Blackberries 73
   in Wine Gelatin 8
Pear Bread 164
   Stew, Lamb and 137
   Pudding 187
Pears with Mint Sorbet 127
Peas, Sugar Snap with Blue Cheese 90
Peppers, Grandmother's 134
Pickle, Watermelon 56
Pineapple-Mint Fantasy 84
Pineapple Rice Salad 72
Piquant Dressing 130
Plum Cake 157
Popovers 34
Poppy Seed Cake 35
   Dressing 172
   Muffins 121
Pork Roast, Stuffed 189
   Spareribs and Sauerkraut 193
Potato Salad, Hot 16
   Soup, Cold 67
Prune Soufflé 194
Pudding, Lemon 38
   Pear 187
   Steamed Cranberry 118
Pumpkin Fruit Cake 141
   Roll, Spicy 114
   Soup 116

R
Raisin Cookies, Low-Sodium 88
Raspberry Dessert, Finnish 185
   Ice 92
Rhubarb Punch 29
   Strawberry Mold 49
   Swirl Dessert 12
Rice Salad, Beet and 99
   and Pineapple 72
Rondeles with Roquefort 122
Rosy Punch 120

S
SALADS
   Antipasto, Tossed 51
   Beans, Marinated Green 61
   Beet and Celery Mold, Jellied 16
      and Rice 99
   Brandade Fish 59
   Broccoli 121
   Coleslaw, Fruit 63
   Cucumber Raita 38
   Garden 91
   Grapefruit, Orange, and Avocado 172
   Green 22
   Greens, Mixed 130

Herring and Macaroni 81
Lettuce 135
Macedoine 5
Orange, Onion, and Black Olive 149
Oriental 126
Potato, Hot 16
Rice and Pineapple 72
Spinach, Lettuce, and Chopped Egg 69
Strawberry Rhubarb Mold 49
Tomato Aspic 155
Tomatoes Stuffed with Cucumbers 117
Tossed, with Sesame 164
Turkey, in Cantaloupe Shells 33
Vegetable, Molded 160
Watercress and Sprouts 138
Zucchini, Marinated 109
   and Pepper 112
SALAD DRESSINGS
   Buttermilk 82
   French 164
   Green 91
   Italian 22
   Paprika 69
   Piquant 130
   Poppy Seed 172
   Spinach 126
   Yogurt 135, 138
Salmon, Bill Davis' Poached 55
   Log 168
SANDWICHES
   Asparagus Rolls, Baked 167
   Chicken, Rolled 133
   Mushroom and Watercress 132
Sauce, Dill 47
   Horseradish 15
   Mustard 15
   Spicy, for Chicken 98
Scalloped Cherry Tomatoes 11
Scallops and Mushrooms, Baked 125
Schrod with Mustard Sauce 11
Scones, Currant 140
   Oatmeal 129
Seafood Newburg 104
Shandy 81
Sherbert, Strawberry 76
Shortbread 27
Shrewsbury Biscuits 79
Shrimp Gumbo 130
Sorbet, Pears with Mint 127
Soufflé, Grits 1
   Lemon 22
   Prune 194
   Roll, Spinach 26
SOUPS
   Asparagus 5

Broccoli 179
Carrot Cream 193
Chicken Watercress 187
Cranberry Borscht 143
Clam Chowder 10
Curry, Cold 33
Fish, Oriental 149
Fishball Chowder 64
Meat and Lentil 183
Potato 67
Pumpkin 116
Tomato Buttermilk 129
Tomato Carrot 14
Zucchini 59
Sour Cream Dessert, Gertrude Fallon's 69
Sour Cream Horseradish Sauce 15
Sour Cream Twists 174
Sour Dough Bread 21
   Bread Sticks 7
   Date-Raisin Coffee Bread 41
   Starter 6
   Streusel Coffee Cake 40
Soused Fish 67
Spaghetti, Nutty 108
Spareribs and Sauerkraut 193
Spiced Curried Beef 37
Spinach and Artichoke Hearts 196
   Baked Onions with 190
   Dressing 126
   Pie 171
   Salad 69
   Soufflé Roll 26
   Squares 147
Spritzer 47
Squash, Stuffed Summer 95
Strawberries 27
   with Angel Food Cake 96
   with Orange Juice and Curaçao 27
   Rhubarb Mold 49
   Sherbert 76
Swedish Ginger Cookies 44
   Pancake 135
Swiss Eggs 40
Syrian Bread 60

T
Tea, Eleanor Fenn's Iced 86
   Spiced Cranberry 140
Three-Grain Bread 134
Toffee Bars 127
Tomato Aspic 155
   Buttermilk Soup 129
   Carrot Soup 14
Tomatoes, Scalloped Cherry 11
   Stuffed with Cucumbers 117

Tongue 15
Tritical Bread 83
Turkey and Oysters, Creamed 144
   Salad 33

V
Vanilla Cookies 77
Vanilla Ice Cream 75
Veal with Water Chestnuts 150
Vegetable Platter, Green 105
Vegetable Salad, Molded 160
VEGETABLES
   Asparagus in Puff Pastry 43
   Artichoke Hearts with Spinach 196
   Brussels Sprouts with Chestnuts 157
   Carrots Malaga 197
   Carrot Casserole 6
   Cucumbers, Freezer 184
      Stuffed Slices 53
   Leeks with Ham 47
   Onions with Spinach, Baked 190
   Peas, Sugar Snap 90
   Sauerkraut, Spareribs and 193
   Spinach and Artichoke Hearts 196
      Baked Onions with 190
      Soufflé Roll 26
   Squash, Stuffed Summer 95
   Tomatoes, Scalloped Cherry 11
      Stuffed with Cucumbers 117
   Vegetable Platter, Green 105

W
Walnut Bars, Frosted 165
Watercress Mushroom Sandwich Filling 132
   Salad 138
   Soup 187
Watermelon Pickle 56
White Bread, Sourdough 6
White Chocolate Mousse 106
Whole Wheat Bread, Quick 194
   Refrigerator Rolls 68
Wine Cooler, Rhine 24

Y
Yogurt Salad Dressing 135, 138
Yorkshire Pudding 156

Z
Zucchini Bread 99
   Chocolate Cake 198
   Drop Cookies 87
   Marinated 109
   and Pepper Salad 112
   Soup, Cold 59

Add more YANKEE BOOKS

The Best Recipes From New England Inns. More than 100 country inns share their traditional favorites and specialties of the house — recipes that have made many of these New England inns famous (and many have never been shared before). From the simple elegance of *Chicken Capiello* (from the Bee and Thistle Inn) to gourmet extravaganzas like *Chez Pierre's Lobster à la Crème* (from the Charlotte Inn) to the chocoholic's fantasy *Black Velvet Cake* (served at The Londonderry Inn), this is a culinary tour of the finest kitchens of the Northeast. You'll find *Fettuccini Tossed with Smoked Native Trout, Chicken Cranberry Kiev* with a surprise filling of tart cranberries and maple syrup, *Blueberry Pie Marnier*, buttery-rich *Scottish Oat Scones, Alan's Coquilles Pêche Royale*, a subtle blending of the flavors of Maine scallops, peaches, and a touch of spice . . . altogether over 330 recipes to bring out the chef in every cook. 320 pages, 6" x 9", hardcover, $15.95

Yankee Magazine's Great New England Recipes and the Cooks Who Made Them Famous. Her fanciest kitchen gadget is a worn blender, and her favorite stove uses oak not kilowatts. Nonetheless, Dorothy Rathbun has earned a reputation as a great cook in her hometown and is just one of the 37 New England cooks featured in this celebration of memorable hometown cookery. From the personal files of cooks who have been featured in *Yankee* Magazine's popular column "Great New England Cooks" comes a wide range of dishes, from ethnic specialties to innovative gourmet cuisine. Included with the more than 300 recipes for appetizers, soups, main dishes, desserts, and breads are fascinating visits with all of the cooks and a generous serving of their cooking secrets. First printing sold out. 320 pages, 6" x 9", hardcover, $15.95

The Clock Watcher's Cookbook, by Judy Duncan and Allison McCance. The hurried cook can still serve great food like *Apple Artichoke Soup* (ready in 20 minutes), *Swiss Scallops* (company fare in only 15 minutes), or elegant *Pork Tenderloin with Cointreau* (prep time 15 minutes), and get out of the kitchen in 60 minutes or less. Cooksaving features include: timetables and complete menus, timesaving appliances and preparation tips, and make-ahead recipes. 128 pages, 6" x 9", comb-bound, indexed, $8.95